Awaken to
YOUR
TRUTH
The Time Is Now

By Joanna Alexopoulos

 FriesenPress

Suite 300 - 990 Fort St
Victoria, BC, V8V 3K2
Canada

www.friesenpress.com

Copyright © 2020 by Joanna Alexopoulos
First Edition — 2020

Mahatma Gandhi
"Be the change you wish to see in the world."

You may contact Joanna Alexopoulos at 1-416-473-4325 or
j_alexopoulos1955@gmail.com for more information about special
discounts for bulk purchases to your organization, for educational
purposes, reselling, book clubs, fundraiser campaigns, gifts or for
any other reason.

You may also visit: www.awaken-to-your-truth.com

ISBN
978-1-5255-5469-8 (Hardcover)
978-1-5255-5470-4 (Paperback)
978-1-5255-5471-1 (eBook)

1. *BODY, MIND & SPIRIT / INSPIRATION & PERSONAL GROWTH*
2. *SELF-HELP / SPIRITUAL*

Distributed to the trade by The Ingram Book Company

CONTENTS

Dedication

To Jeselina
My Earth angel
Who inspired me to see the greatness that I am
Who gave me strength and courage to carry on
Who understood me like no other
Who trusted me and gave me hope
Who never gave up on me
Who showed me the truth
I love you

Introduction

My life, I must admit, has been an interesting and most incredible journey thus far, one which I will share with you, in part.

I am a channeler of love, peace and compassion for humanity. I channel messages from the Divine realms of existence, from universal intelligence, through a form of communication called automatic writing.

I came across this gift after a lifetime of pain and suffering. My search for clarity led to my quest and thirst for knowledge of the unknown, in an attempt to understand myself—in an attempt to heal myself. I learnt about life, about God/Universe, and about the life beyond. I came to understand about energy, vibration, and frequency. I learnt about how the universe functions, and the connection that there is to all.

Through this quest, I discovered I am an empath. I am highly sensitive to the feelings and emotions of others and to the energetic imbalances of our world. Being this sensitive made it difficult to live a *normal* life. I was different, trying to fit in, to a world that was not like me. I was oblivious to the gifts I had. I was oblivious to who I really am. I am still learning about myself and ways to better manage my sensitivities, to be more present and use these abilities for the highest good of all.

I spent most of my life in darkness, unknowingly absorbing the pain of others. I suffered in silence, not understanding who I was, ill and alone, in despair .... frustrated, angry and confused. I struggled emotionally feeling helpless, hopeless, alienated, and afraid. I struggled physically with shallow breathing, weakness, chronic fatigue, headache, poor vision, nausea, brain fog and heaviness in my heart.

I discovered myself through my awakening, when my suffering had reached its peak, when I had had enough after five decades of forceful suppression. I felt the end was near in 2012. It was at this time that Divinity spoke to me through my spirit guides, Jacob and Emmanuel.

I was led to communicate through automatic writing. I followed my intuition, took a pen and paper, and set my intention. I was deeply touched by this experience. Overwhelmed with emotion, I wept in silence. It was at this time that faith and hope within me renewed itself. I knew I was not alone.

My guides, angels, and guardians gave me message after message of encouragement, and these became louder and louder. I was guided to Abadania, Brazil and in November 2017, I courageously took this trip in faith and in trust. This was the turning point of my life. It was at this time that my consciousness shifted. The benevolent entities performed a spiritual release which paved the way to deeper understandings and new more elevated experiences.

Awaken To Your Truth: The Time Is Now began its journey in March 2018. This book was not written by me. It was written through me. I allowed myself to be an open conduit for higher wisdom to flow, through me and onto my pages. I accepted, incorporated and transcribed what came through as a narrative—a thought-provoking piece, to serve humanity in the biggest way.

I live my life with gratitude, in a peaceful and humbling state. My life has been a struggle, but no experience is ever wasted. I am grateful that my challenges have led to where I am today. With deep compassion for our world, I assist in the awakening process of our species.

Through this book, I wish to inspire, encourage and support all who wish to better themselves, all who wish to understand the deeper meaning of life, all who wish to take the responsibility to heal our world, and all who are suffering their own private battles and who believe there is no other way. There is always hope. There is always a better way.

Awaken To Your Truth: The Time Is Now shows us how to access and activate the innate truth of who we are—that which will bring us out of our personal and global darkness. It is an urgent plea to humanity to awaken to the world that we have created and begin our inner work, for transcendence.

There is no need for pain and suffering. There is need for love and humility. Love is All That Is and it is love that will heal all.

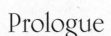

Prologue

Ascended Masters reveal:

We are ascended masters of the ninth dimension. We are highly evolved beings who have lived on the earth plane and are now in the highest realm in the life beyond, the everlasting life of universal love. We have chosen to collectively assist you in understanding basic concepts that you have forgotten. We have been sent to you by God to encourage, support, inspire and awaken you to the truth of who you are, to assist you in your path of rediscovery in an attempt in healing yourselves and your planet. We come with purity and love for all, to lead the way in your self-discovery. We are everywhere and with everyone.

We speak to you at this time for this is the time of new beginnings. We wish to deliver messages that will create movement for grander advancements. We have walked on earth and know your (humanity's) pain. We see you. We feel you. We love you and want to help you. Our messages are of love and light.

Light essences of crystallized forms are penetrating the consciousness of your species at this time, with thoughts of highest form and inspiration, to facilitate the shift that will transform you, to live a life that is free from the egoic state that is contributing to the demise of your species.

Living in your world has not been an easy one. It is time to regain your focus. It is time to slow down and think more clearly on where you are and where you are going with the life that you are now leading.

This book will clarify what it is you need to know, and what it is you need to do, to get out of your minds and into your hearts, to create the change you desperately want, in order to live your lives more fully. It will show you the way, out of the darkness and into the light and wonder of the oneness of who you really are.

It is written to act as a catalyst for change, to alter the very fabric of your existence, to provide food for thought, for contemplation.

You all want the same. You want love, peace and harmony. The time is now to create the shift to set this in motion.

Let it be known what you will read is wisdom of All That Is. The words on these pages are channeled energy from the God that you know, for there is only one and He loves you deeply.

Time has come
To awaken one another
In remembrance of who we are
One family

Time has come
To recognize our ability
In unwavering potentiality
The light that we may bring

Time has come
To lift ourselves up
In remembrance of
The Divinity that we are

1
Who Are You?

There is a universal force which unifies all. Some may wish to call this force God, others Creator, the Universe, Source, The All Knowing, or All That Is. Labeling this truth causes separation. There is no need.

In the limited conscious mind, there is a need to label, categorize and compare. There is an innate need to separate in order to substantiate the need for isolation. Life is not meant to be compartmentalized.

Life is inclusive not subjective. It is matter interacting with the frequencies of what one vibrates. Life is a mirror of what one puts forth ... a replay of thought forms and feelings that one emanates. And it is the emergence of these energies collectively that vibrate in one unified field of consciousness that brings all life forms together, amplifying and exhibiting where you and your species are, as a whole, at this time.

You are one ball of energy creating and co-creating your reality, your world, together. You are vibrating as one, interconnected and interdependent upon one another.

The unity that you are as a collective is a concept that needs to be understood at the fundamental level—an important concept that will assist your species in awakening to your truth.

The time is now to begin the process of expanding your consciousness, in moving forward and upward from where you are at this time.

You are moving out of your materialistic, egoic self into a more ascended self, whereby you may attain peace and harmony—the peace and harmony that you are longing for. There is no greater time than now.

Have faith in knowing you are being assisted greatly.

An energetic movement towards more advanced creative thinking is being poured onto your planet and into the minds of those most open. It is elevating the consciousness of many. This powerful energy is impacting and influencing you to a higher awareness. It is elevating you to greater heights, to spread this wisdom to the minds of the masses, to see what you haven't seen and do what you haven't done, to finally have clarity.

More and more of you are coming into newer understandings. More and more are awakening to the truth of who you are.

Your species is undergoing an awakening ... an awakening to the truth of its creations. New concepts and understandings are fostering and permeating shifts towards new awareness for growth and expansion.

Your time is now to unite, to come together and realize the grand potential of who you are, to create a movement of transcendence that will free you and your home from the suffering states that you are in—free yourselves from the limitations set before you, by your minds.

The time is now to understand fully that which you are, the power that you have, and the action you may take to return to yourselves your very *selves*—to assist in the healing of your planet.

Since the beginning of time, man has concerned himself with matters of little importance, from the needs to the wants, losing himself from the reality of his true essence—the reality of who he is in the purest form.

Your species has transformed itself into something that is not, something that is more inhumane in its entirety.

Advancements in technology have allowed for growth, but in ways that are not supporting you. It is this that shall destroy. It is this that has ruptured the humanness out of humanity, used as an escape from reality, a reason to withdraw, to lose yourselves to the delusion of false realities created not by free will but by the pull of forces beyond your control.

You are not what you have made yourselves out to be. You are not without emotion.

Humanity has withdrawn its humanness and has become robotic and disengaged in its acts of violence, greed, and self-destruction, mirroring what it perceives as truths, continuing in the cycle of selfish demise. The time is now to wake up.

There have been writers and speakers, artists and musicians, filmmakers and poets putting forth messages to you ... messages of awareness, messages from spirit, longing for you to see the light ... messages from God.

The time is now to awaken. The time is now to awaken to the potentiality of who you are, to live your lives more fully, in the grace of who you are. The time is now to act to bring yourselves back to the balance that you all need.

The biggest truth of life lies within the domain of continual survival. Being in physicality allows you to create. This is your purpose: to live to your fullest, experiencing, learning, growing, and evolving. You are on an evolutionary path of development, attracting to you whatever it is that you wish. You are the magnets of your reality, and the reality of your world as a collective.

This is your truth, and this is what you need to realize and make use of fully.

Your species has unconsciously fallen victim to your own constructions, living a life that is beyond your control. Your idealistic perception has led to separation—separation of yourselves from your own creations. This is what is destroying you and your home. You are not living consciously.

The belief there is the power of the mind—the analytical, critical-thinking mind—that is influencing the direction of the outcome of your realities is (in essence) the actual truth.

Understand fully, it is also the power of the mind—the ego mind—that is bringing your species down a destructive path, drawing to you the powerful forces of regret, greed, deception, and malice.

It is time to understand that you are not your mind. Your species has lost yourselves.

The mind in itself is an organ that breathes the existence of your thinking patterns in allowance for informed decisions, in the execution of future realities.

As much as your mind is of use to you, it is to the determent of the existence of your authentic self. Allowing this control, which your mind has on you, to reign and foster impedes on the allowance of the soul self to nurture and develop.

It is the mere existence and reign of the egoic mind that rules in today's society. This is what has brought your species to its knees. It is a painful reality, being caught up with a false reality as the game of life, the game of accumulation of things, material things that bring no joy but merely egoic satisfaction of accomplishment.

It is the *you* who is not the real *you* that has the power over you. It is the delusion of false realities that has its grips on your species, for this is what you have allowed.

Confusion, uncertainty, and anxiety foster your decisions. You are forcing your way into your tomorrows.

Take the time to sit, breathe, and feel to bring yourselves to a place of clarity—clarity that will bring forth new insights for better tomorrows.

Take the time that you need. There is no greater power than the power that is within you. You all have time, for there is not much time needed apart from the time of pure intent and focus. Time restricts one from being. Sit, breathe, and digest to have the clarity that you are yearning.

Manifestation of realities is a God-given gift. It is within you to create and co-create, for this is why you came: to create the world you choose to live in, to create with the power that is within you. Bring to your awareness what you have created in your world. Notice and observe. Is this what you really want?

When you take a moment to reflect, you may be saddened. You may be saddened by the creations of your species' reality. You may be saddened by the creations of the reality of your choosing.

What you have created for yourselves and together as one unified collective is not something that you would consciously choose for yourselves. Your realities are bleak. The world around you is suffering. Your species has lost your way.

Rest assured there is hope. All can be reversed. There is always hope. You are eternal beings with great powers.

The time is now to rejoice, to come to full realization of who you truly are, and use your innate power to create the shift that will move you upward and onward to new beginnings of hope and promise—of love. The time is now to assist in the evolution of your planet.

You must slow down to do this. You need to slow down to feel, as this is who you truly are. You are the soul that lies within you and around you, connecting you to everyone and everything in your planet. You are one universal force, longing to re-unite in the beauty of this oneness. Believe this as this is the truth.

Living with the belief that situations are out of your control, and expecting others to harmonize your personal and global problems, is not living at all. This is living in the falsehood of the delusion you are creating. You are sleeping in your own unconsciousness. This in itself is separation, and this will not bring peace and harmony. You are not separate from your world. This is the reality.

Awaken to your truth that God is one universal intelligence that is within each and every one of you. You are not separate from Him or from one another. You are living in the illusion of separateness. This is what is creating all of your problems.

You are one—one family living together in your home, which you call Earth. You are within God's family in physical form, experiencing yourselves with the beauty of all your senses. Live consciously to fully access and utilize what God has given you. Get out of your minds and into your hearts.

Many of your species live unconsciously. They are suffering greatly, and their suffering is creating suffering for others. Understand that you are all connected and thus affected by one another.

In preparation for clarity, you must slow down. You must breathe and digest what you are experiencing in your lives and what you see in your world.

You are not alone. You are not separate from each other. Alter your thinking to change your lives. Begin to see the beauty of this truth. It is within you to assist in raising the vibration of your planet to create a movement that will uplift you. This is within your reach. The choice is yours.

The fear of God is keeping many of you in this state of separateness, keeping you in a false state of individualized thinking. It is easier to pass the blame onto others. It is easier to not take responsibility. Those who blame are those who are lost in the deception of their own false thinking patterns.

Look within and take responsibility to open your hearts to the understanding of unity and transcendence. Blame holds one hostage to the truth of who you are. It is this low vibrational thinking that has brought your species to this state. It is your ego mind holding you where it is safe, where it is comfortable, as this is all that it knows from a lifetime of habitual patterning.

Recognize that you are not this limitation. Anything that is outside you that is holding you back is not what is real. What is inside you is what is real. Spend more time within to create the stillness that you need to understand yourselves more fully. You want things to improve. This is how to improve them.

Accept this truth and confirm to yourselves that you are absolute beings with unlimited power that may transcend all obstacles. The time is now to access your power.

It is within you to assist in the implementation of the transformation that is so vitally important—the transformation that will awaken your species to its present reality. Take charge and do your part to collectively create an entire collaboration of healing for your planet. The time is now.

There is hope—hope for your future, whereby your expanded consciousness will bring you to greater insights and opportunities, which will facilitate the creation of a world free from injustice, free from inequity, free from pain, and free from the false paradigm of old belief systems that reinforce "it is out of my control," for you, each and every one of you, is in ultimate control of your realities.

As a collective, your species tends to wait for others to fix your problems. Do not wait for others. Do not wait for God to intervene. Do not believe that God will take you out of your misery, your pain, and your suffering states.

God is unconditional love. God is compassion. God is forgiveness.

God has given you the greatest gift of all: the gift of creativity, allowing you the freedom to explore and bring forth the greatest experiences of your choosing. God sees the light in each and every one of you. It is in this truth that He will not intervene, as all of this is of your own choosing.

The time is now to accept all as it is and take responsibility. The time is now to have faith in knowing you can make a change. The time is now to know that you can surpass all obstacles and grow from wherever it is you are at this time. The time is now to understand the Godly nature in you.

Begin from a place of stillness. Feel. Allow yourselves the time to feel your emotions, to begin to heal and transcend them, to create the shift that is awaiting you, to expand your consciousness, and come to new insights and understandings that will give you the clarity of where you are now and where you are going. Your future is bright with promise and glory with the innate truth that you are beginning to realize within yourselves.

The time is now to heal yourselves. The power is within you. The time is now to heal yourselves and heal your world.

The time is now to take responsibility and take charge of what you are collectively creating and experiencing.

Teach your children to love themselves, to accept who they are in the greatness of who they are. Honor their differences, their strengths, and their weaknesses. Do not judge, do not compare, and do not label for this is what is crippling the very essence of who your children are. Celebrate their contributions big and small, for they are all in their creative processes, just as each and every one of you.

Your school systems have fostered curriculums based on individual survival of the fittest. This is not supporting the light and love that you are. This is not in alignment with your truth. It is in line with the fear-based perspective of separation, which you are not.

Competition separates and crushes. The survival of the self dominates in your schools with disregard for the unity of the collective. Educators follow this philosophy blindly, for they know not another way. They dare not to challenge. They dare not have a voice. It is easier not to.

You are all in this game of life together. Realize this to exercise it. You are no greater, not superior to any other. You are all unique. You are all special.

Teach your children the values of leadership. Teach them the importance of morality. Teach them to make decisions from a loving heart, which will not only benefit the few but the collective, for it is in these children that transformation shall prevail.

The time is now to change your minds and change your ways to create movement towards higher understandings of life and the unity of all in existence.

Your species has led itself down a pathway of self-destruction. Your focus has primarily been on the individual self and its personal world. You are living your lives apart from others. You tend to believe in the immunity of the creations of others, and you place blame on others for where you collectively are at this time. You have been living but not really living. You have merely been existing, going through the motions of life.

The time is now to remember that it is in your power to live a more meaningful and fulfilling life. The time is now to recognize that you can attain anything you wish to attain without struggle ... with peace, love, and harmony. Allow yourselves this gift. Allow yourselves to experience this elevated consciousness while still in your physical states—while still in this lifetime.

You are supported by a greater power. You are not alone. You are never alone. Beings of higher intelligence are around you, supporting you, honoring the light that you are, lovingly guiding you from wherever it is that you are, without judgment. Angels are all around you, assisting you in your choices, inspiring you, and encouraging you. You are not alone.

The time is now to stop living as you have been, to stop living so unconsciously. See life as the gift that it is. See yourselves working with your world to create a better one for you. See yourselves working together, uniting in the oneness of who you really are. You are connected by a greater power. You are connected to God.

There need not be suffering. The power lies within you, and it all begins by altering your beliefs about you.

The competitive nature that prevails in your societies is crippling the very essence of who you are.

Realize you are perfection. You are nothing less. The time is now to gain new, more elevated understandings to support your growth and support your transformation, which will enable you to see more clearly. The time is now to awaken to the *you* that you have forgotten.

Your youth has a wider awareness of what it is that is damaging the nature of your species. They see the destructive patterning that ignorance has created. They see the bigger picture, and they rejoice in creating movements for change—change that will benefit all of you, change that will benefit your species and your planet. They see what you have yet to see.

Your species is in crisis. Your planet is dying. It is vital to raise your awareness. You need to awaken from your dormancy states. You need to awaken and take ownership of what you have created as a collective.

Pressure is put upon you. Protests and revolutions remind you. Your world is suffering. The time is now to take a stand, to pool together and take ownership for the chaotic nature of your world. You are all in this together.

Understand you can make a difference, for you are a part of something much greater. You are not separate. The biggest misconception is that you are.

Understand fully that you are one unified field connected to the universal light of Divine essence of love and truth, of Divine intelligence. You are of God, not separate from Him or from each other. What you do to yourselves, you do to all.

Take more care of yourselves to make a difference. Love yourselves, to create movement for change. Love will bring your species together. Be in preparation to assist the masses. With love in your hearts, with love as the driving force, transformation will inevitably prevail, and this will bring you back to yourselves, to the love of who you are, and to the unity of all in existence.

World leaders will falter. Those in power will no longer lead. The corruption that has been prevalent in your civilizations will no longer suffocate its people. Stand together to see this happen. The time is now.

Having given up your power to those in authority has not served you. Greed and self-righteousness are what drive them. Without the morality behind their decisions, without love in their hearts, there will never be a change that will be for the people. Awaken to this truth.

It is time to wake up to the world you have collectively created. It is time to take responsibility.

Your species tends to be in a place of judgment. This is what is prevalent in your societies. There is criticism, and there is judgment. There is comparison of what you have and what you are. You live with regret and disappointment. Your species is lost. You have lost your way.

Do not judge your leaders and neither condemn them. Do not be in judgment, for you are all creating your experiences and your realities together. Regain your power, your control, and make your lives what you want it to be, for every single one of you is in absolute control.

The time is now to take back your power.

Your species is in a state of delusion. Subconsciously this has served you well. It has allowed you to live your lives as you independently wish to experience it. This delusional state has also allowed you to forget. There is little compassion in your world. There is little care for one another. There is selfishness and self-centered thinking. This is a truth that hurts you all.

Living in a society without compassion is living in a reality without substance. There is nothing but emptiness. There is a void amongst you. There tends to be no emotion for what your species do to each other. There tends to be no emotion for what you do to yourselves. This is the sad truth. This is the reality that you have to face and to alter.

The time is now. Fully realize that you are the biggest creators of all, and you can change everything.

Maintaining the peace that you are—maintaining the essence of who you are—will bring you to new beginnings in an effort to establish the groundwork necessary for peaceful resolution. Forcefully impacting ways that may bring about a movement of transition will only anger the masses and create more injustice in your world.

Without doubt, forces of nature will impact you greatly, and this in itself will shake you into the realization of your creations and the need for change. It is inevitable that your world is crumbling, as you continue to live your lives unconsciously.

Take the time to observe and absorb what you see around you. What you hear on your news reminds you of the catastrophic nature of your species. Come to the realization that you have taken part in this. Energy is collective, and you are all of this energy.

Beginning as a seed
Planting its roots
Into the darkness
Yearning to find its way

Glorifying the beauty
Of its soul creation
As it burns with desire
To burst into its wonder

2
You Hold the Power

Behold the truth of your existence. You are in physicality to evolve, to nurture your creations, and to manifest new, wonderful beginnings.

Your species is living a lifestyle with attitudes that are causing you to forget who you are. Choosing to think the way you do, speak the way you do, manage your lives the way you do is suppressing your consciousness from seeing the truth of the potentiality of who you are. You are living unconsciously. You are choosing a lifestyle which is not supporting you.

Take the time to be in this remembrance. Pause long enough to think and contemplate. This will assist in the breakthrough you need to understand that your thinking patterns, belief systems, and attitudes foster your creations. This will bring you out of your world of darkness. It will bring you into the light.

Trust that you are in control, and you can make the changes that are necessary.

The time has come to move forward and upward and fully embrace the beauty of who you are.

Look within to find your answers. Make the transition into looking within yourselves to not only clear the pathway to higher concepts and understandings but to also place yourselves into full gear, ready to embark on new developments. Accept where you are at this time and take responsibility, to allow yourselves to be a conduit through which higher possibilities may filter.

We are so very pleased many of you have come to this realization.

Bring yourselves to this awareness. With more and more of you in understanding, more and more will collectively align.

Your world needs assistance. It is crying out for help. There is too much sadness. There is too much violence. There is too much aggression—too much turmoil. There is chaos in your world. Believe this as the truth of who you are at this time.

This state of non-compliance to the Divine in you is creating the existence that your species most fears. Humanity is lost. You have lost yourselves in your creations, living your lives without purpose, without substance, without joy. The grief, the frustration, and the dysfunction of your world has reached its peak. The time is now to understand that it is in your power to change this.

Come to the basic truth that you are not separate. You are not removed. Only then may you see the light—the light of new beginnings that will enhance your growth and save your planet.

Your species is in a primitive state of existence, moving out of the egoic self-sabotaging stage towards the magical and enlightened stages of evolution. Your species is in transition, with more and more of you in understanding of deeper truths.

Your world has come to a destructive peak. Many are at a stalemate, barely functioning, living in physical form with a body and a mind yet not in awareness of what this means and what blessings this brings.

Rejoice in the truth of who you are and the absolute joy this brings, being offered the opportunity to live in flesh and experience life fully.

Take more time to be with yourselves, to sooner come to the clarity you need of what your world has become and the role you have played and are playing living in it.

The time is now. You are not separate, in and of each other, and you are not alone in this universe. You are connected to All That Is.

Make it a priority to live your lives more consciously. Be more mindful of how you are living. Wake each morning knowing you are well supported. Practice gratitude. Count your blessings for there are many. Focus on all that you are and all that you have and live with gratitude in your hearts.

Your planet is suffering. The chaos in your world will continue for as long as you remain in your dormancy. Your home is not in good balance. It is trying to cope with all the suffering of your species and its destructive patterning. It is struggling to rebalance and sustain itself.

More and more of you will witness global disturbances in your world. There will be an increase in warfare. Disputes will peak and explode into major upheavals. There will be an increase in natural disasters in various forms and with greater intensities.

Powerful forces of destruction are coming your way in an attempt by Mother Earth to rebalance herself and renew the life-force energy that she needs for continual survival. All within her path will waver and pass, but all in the goodness of renewed faith and understanding. Inevitable restructuring must prevail. Old patterns must be replaced with new patterns. This is your reality.

There is disturbance in the natural order of life. You all see this but many ignore. You know things are changing with your weather patterns but many ignore. You begrudge Mother Nature for delivering you outcomes not to your liking.

Understand climate change is affecting you at every level. The impact it will have on you is of great magnitude.

The time is now to wake up and take responsibility for what your species as a collective has created. It is in your power to think again and create the shift that is necessary to restore the balance of your planet before further damage causes it non-compliance. Do your part in creating a transference of energy that will shift you into new, more pleasing directions.

Assist in the healing of your planet. There is an expectation amongst you that fosters the belief that others must take action. This is not how it is.

Be in remembrance of who you are and why you came here.

Disruption and unease permeate at this time. The time is now to create the shift that you have all been awaiting, to bring you to greater heights and understandings.

We have come to you now to restore the hope within you, and to support you in reversing what you believe to be your destiny. We are here to assist you in making a shift from this state of delusion towards your awakening, to bring you out of your despair in preparation for a movement that will foster your growth, not suppress it any further.

The time is now. Be in this remembrance that you are the power whereby anything is possible. You are infinite beings of love and light with unlimited power. You may restore the balance within yourselves and within your world. You can restore it all.

We wish you to relax into this thinking, and just for a few moments, digest all that we have put forth in the first few pages. Digest it all. Take a moment to soak it all in, as you owe it to yourselves to do so.

Honor yourselves as you are the God spirit that lies within, and you are the power that can heal your world. This is the very truth of who you are.

We are here to assist you in this transition. We are here to remind you of who you are.

Be in this remembrance to bring about newfound, much-needed insight to your species. In God's creations, you are His most prized members, as it is you whom He has given the gift that allows you to be who and what you choose to be. With a mind and a body, you can create and you can experience.

With this knowledge moving forward comes the responsibility in knowing you were created equal to one another. There is no one being that is superior to any other, as God has created you equal. Once understood, this becomes a painful realization of the truth— the truth in realizing you have not been kind to yourselves, to each other, nor to what supports you.

Your species is lacking the love that binds you. You are not in sync with the love of who you are.

Publicly acclaimed are those who do not falter in the eyes of your masses. Your public figures are adored and respected by many. In reality, it is they who are suppressing the very fabric of your existence. This is all in the darkness that you have fallen into. It is all too easy to follow suit, to follow the norm, to not have to think. It is all too difficult to think for yourselves.

Now let us stop for a moment to contemplate. Let us confirm ... your species does not think for yourselves ... but you think you do.

Your institutions, whether they are religious, political, economic, educational, or social in nature, are the ones that think for you. What your species does is follow.

You are not here, in this physical existence, to follow. You are here to think for yourselves and to move forward in your creative processes through life. You have all that you need within you. Within this remembrance lies the truth of who you are.

There is no time like the present to be in the remembrance that you are in complete control of your lives. You can move forward knowing that there is nothing that you cannot be, do, or have. You can move forward understanding that all is within your power to bring to you all of what you are longing for. The power is within you once you understand fully the simple yet profound basic truths of the universe.

All that you have accumulated with the power of your minds, and the focus that is not within your hearts, has without a doubt transformed your existence into isolated, resistant micro-beings, managed by those in superior powers, whose ultimate goals are not the common good for humanity but rather individualistic, authoritarian dictatorship, accumulating more and more to satisfy their own needs and wants, without the care and concern for the collective. This is the bitter truth—the truth that many already know yet continue to ignore.

Your species is living in an unconscious state with the perception of powerlessness.

Being in this state compels you to be without free will. It inhibits the truth to activate and permeate ... to bring forth insights that will develop and assist in the evolutionary consciousness of your planet. It is unfortunate that so many are plagued by this deception, in the unknowingness and falsehoods of your realities.

Pay more attention to what is happening in your world. Take the time to fully understand what is happening. This will allow insight to come through, to plant its seeds, which will foster new beginnings for your entire species.

Consider being in the forefront, having the power to manage yourselves in loving and compassionate ways without the anxiety and bitterness of competition and glory, without your egoic selves competing for recognition. Feel for a moment the energy of unification, of oneness with God—oneness with who you truly are. Feel as this is who you are. This peace and love and compassion that dwells within you is who you are. Understand this to begin to see the light in you that will change your world.

Move forward, trusting that it is within you to create a movement towards empowerment. Take the time to stop and feel. Go within. This is where you will find the peace and serenity of your soul. This is where you will unlock the tools for compassion and love to rule your lives and your home.

Bring forth your talents, skills, and all your knowledge. Come together in peace and in harmony as a united force and create the existence that is yours to create with balance, with love, and with compassion for one another and for all on your planet.

It is you who are the doers, you who have the power in your physical states, consciousness in form. This is why you came here.

Your conditioned past has crippled your species into thinking and believing that there are certain aspects of yourselves and your lives that have not been of your choosing. You believe you have not brought them into your reality as this cannot be the truth.

As there are certain aspects of your realities that have been brought to you from other lifetimes carrying through, you most certainly can move them into more positive directions. You can transcend past these limitations.

Subconsciously, aspects of your lives are brought forth for you to look at more deeply. Look at them to surpass them. Allow them to pass through you to be cleansed, cleared, and released from your consciousness so that you can move forward and upward on your evolutionary scale of development. There is no need to hang onto past residual negative energy that is holding you back, suppressing you from living fully in the life that you have now.

The time is now to understand this is not who you are. You are not your past.

You are supreme beings with unlimited potentiality. Live in the truth of who you are, knowing that you are not your past, you are not who you were in any other lifetimes. You are not your conditioned past of who you were in your childhood or adolescence or at any other time in your past. Whatever you have experienced, from a lifetime of being told who you are, is not who you are today ... unless you choose to be.

You are here to make a difference in this lifetime. You are here to move out of the chains of your past.

To do this you must practice awareness. Be more mindful of how you are living your lives. You must practice patience. Be still to find the inner peace that you are longing for, that will enable you to experience the pure joy and love of who you are in its entirety. You must practice diligence and commitment.

Trust in the truth of who you are. You have the ultimate potential and the ultimate tools that will assist you in your evolution and in the evolution of your species. You have merely not accessed them.

You are greatness, and you have the greatest potential to be and experience the most magnificent model of yourselves. It is in your power and in your control to manifest this reality. Make the simple shift into awareness. Bring yourselves to where you need to be at this time. The time is now. The time has come to transcend into higher concepts and understandings.

A planetary shift is happening now. Many are experiencing great disturbances within themselves. Many are wanting to know more about who you are, why you came—wanting to understand the deeper meaning of life.

You are ready to grow and we are assisting you by providing you with downloads of higher frequency activations.

Many of you are in wanting of something else. You are tired of the injustices in your world. You are tired of the old paradigm of dysfunction. Intuitively you know there is much more. You are beginning to see the light. You are beginning to awaken to the truth of who you are.

Clarity will follow.

Divine support is waiting for each of you. It will be noticed and utilized. You are going through a process of growth and expansion.

Believe in who you are as the infinite potentiality, for it is only when you see yourselves in this way that you will begin to understand your unlimited potential. The time has come to grasp this very concept.

In this remembrance, you will hold the power and assist one another to be in this place of remembrance. With love in your hearts, all will liberate and unfold as it should, unlocking the hidden keys and hidden truths that lie dormant deep within you.

Living as you have been has allowed you the freedom to live your lives separately. Realize that this is not who you are. Your world is not functioning. Your species has lost itself in the imbalance that you have created. This unconscious living has suppressed the very essence of who you are—the Godly nature in you.

It is with this forgetfulness that we come to you to assist you at this time.

Being in a physical body enables you to experience—to feel. This is why you came: to feel through your experiences that which you choose to actively bring forth into your reality. This is a conscious effort on your part. It is you who has this power to choose what you wish to attract into your lives.

It is you who has chosen the life that you lead. It is you who has chosen the conflicts that you are faced with. It is all in your inner self, in who and what you have chosen to be to enhance your souls, to evolve as Divine beings.

Without conflict, there can be no resolution. Without darkness, there can be no light. Without negative experiences, there can be no positives, for this is the life that you are living, in the duality of all in existence. It is you who has chosen all that you see before you, all the good and the bad, all the happy and the sad, all the right and the wrong as you perceive them. It is you.

Challenges and obstacles will present themselves. It is only in this way that you may move forward to experience the joy of why you came. Without the negative, there can be no positive. You need to experience the darkness for there to be light, to know yourselves more fully. Remember you are in physical form to feel, to experience and feel, in order to understand. This is a very basic concept of who you are.

This may bring you into remembrance. You may see life differently. You may understand and fully accept your experiences not as the darkness but as the light of your becoming. You may embrace the darkness, for only then may there be light. Being in resistance will bring forth more pain and more suffering.

As difficult as it is to grasp, this is your reality. This is how life works. Understanding this truth will set you free. It will bring you new opportunity for growth.

We encourage you to take these words and deeply come to the remembrance of who you are. We encourage you to come to the realization of who you truly are, for it is only in this realization that you may experience the Divine nature in you.

Your species has lost its way. You are destroying yourselves and your entire existence. Your planet is suffering. This is not your purpose. Along with the darkness, comes the light. There is hope.

Contemplate for a moment how it would be if all worked together, if all cooperated and assisted each other, if all understood the unity of all in existence.

When there is unity, there is peace and harmony. There is no room for suffering. This is the ultimate reality of that which you can create. It is in your power to manifest this beautiful truth.

Love will bring you together. Accept one another with your differences. You are all different yet the same. You are of the same essence. You see yourselves as separate but you are not. You are all connected, creating your world together as you see it, and you all see it differently.

Unite with love in your hearts and accept one another. You have a commonality amongst you that you cannot see. You are made of the same fabric. Put aside your differences and see yourselves as one. Unite to save yourselves and your planet.

Without contemplation, there can be no resolution. Think again when you have doubt. Trust in the ultimate potentiality of who you are. Remember this truth, to bring yourselves back to yourselves.

We have planted the seeds for this much-needed shift to permeate on your planet. More and more are awakening to this awareness. This is the time to unite. Do not resist. This is the time to set aside your egos and work with each other to bring not only yourselves but your planet back into alignment.

Put aside your differences. Your beliefs are separating you, and your beliefs are destroying you. They are creating experiences that are not in line with who you are. Let go of what you believe to be right and wrong. There is no right or wrong. It is all in what your beliefs are telling you. When you understand who you are at a deep level you will live your lives with what supports you.

Believe only what is true in your heart. God does not want you to suffer. God is not vengeful. He is not angry. He does not want you to be subjected to violence, fear, lack, or loss. He does not want you to be subjected to any limitation. God wants you to have the freedom to live without restrictions and judgments. God loves you without conditions. He does not need or want anything from you.

God is complete and so are you. You have merely forgotten. We are here to remind you. Stop believing what you hear. Think for yourselves. God is pure love and light. This is what God is.

Create the life that is meant for you to create. It is in your power to live fully in full alignment with your soul. The choice is yours. God has given you this gift of creation. Think again and take yourselves out of your suffering states. Respect one another with your differences to foster the God essence in you.

Understand fully that you are Source energy beings in physical form to manifest the life of your choosing. You are Divine beings, and as such are in total control of your realities as you can direct them.

Awaken to this understanding. You are nothing less than purity and excellence. We cannot stress this enough. You are in a wondrous state of optimizing your experiences on the earth plane, and you have this lifetime to do it, for this is the lifetime that you are experiencing at this time.

You are compassionate beings. Return to the love that you are. Resist the hurt and the blame and the attachments of guilt, shame, greed, and fear, for it is these low vibrational states that have brought your species to its catastrophic existence.

Fully understand you are in total control.

With awareness comes responsibility, which your species has not taken, responsibility in understanding that the global situation is as it is because of the choices that you have collectively made. Take responsibility to bring forth new insights into fully realizing and embracing your potentiality. As beings of light, you may foster growth and opportunity. It is in your power to do so.

Despair not, leave no mark
Never forgotten
Surrender the darkness
Move into the spark of all creation
For therein lie your answers

3
Your Beliefs Are Killing You

Throughout history, religion has served to create community, and it served you well. It is time to recognize the difference between living in a community that fosters fear and living in a community that supports individuality, unity, and love.

Throughout history, man has wondered, yearning to find the truth, living within his insecurities, wondering what it is that he must do to be in the perfection that he must be to please God, for fear of abandonment, for fear of retribution, everlasting pain, and suffering, for fear of eternal death.

Throughout the evolution of humanity, religion has gained more and more power with its self-indulgent desires in keeping its solidarity, while at the same time, suppressing the individuality and self-expression of its members.

Organized religion once had its place. The time has come to understand that its views, misinterpretations, and intentions have contributed to the disempowerment perspective of lack in your species.

It is time to understand that religion does not have complete understandings. It is limited in its thinking. It has not been allowed to grow.

There is more to know. We are here to remind you.

Your religions have steered you wrongly. They have crippled your belief in Source, the light of who you are. They live in fear of losing control, and their fear is projected back onto you.

This is extreme. We know we are shaking your beliefs at this time, but this is the time that your beliefs must be shaken and re-evaluated. It is time to re-evaluate what you have been choosing.

Many will challenge what we have presented, and rightfully so, for this is all that you know. This has been the mindset of many. You have given up your power in allowance for others to control you.

It is time to question. It is time to question the purpose of your religions. God is unconditional love. God is unity. God loves you all.

Look around. Do you see unity? Do you see love for humanity? What is it that you see? Contemplate. What is it that your organized faiths have created?

Your faiths have fostered fear, competition, separation … disempowerment.

They preach unity but deliver division. They preach love but deliver fear. They preach hope but deliver lack.

This dependency has not supported your growth. It is time to awaken and begin the process of thinking for yourselves.

It is not death that you must fear. It is life—this life that you have collectively created. This is the death that you must fear: the death of your mere existence.

Recognize that there is chaos in your world. There is anger, intolerance, hatred, prejudice, and injustice of all kinds. Recognize the direct role that religion has played and how it has contributed to this chaos. Recognize how beliefs of superiority have supported separation, inequity, and corruption.

More and more are awakening to this reality. Your species is coming into the understanding of what has served you and what hasn't. Judgment and criticism are not bringing people together. More and more are questioning, wondering about the truth in all of this, for this cannot be what God wants.

With separation, there cannot be unity. There is only fear. Solidarity holds its bearings in this belief of superiority. There is confusion amongst you. There is a loss of self and a loss of love. Your species has little love for yourselves, nor for one another.

You believe in the truth that you have been told. This is what has been conditioned into your minds. This is what has been ingrained into your psyche by your parents, by your leaders, and by your communities.

Understand that there is no one faith that is better or greater than the other. There is no one faith that is superior. It is time to understand this, to open yourselves up to greater understandings, to return to the love and the peace that you are.

Trust and believe that God loves you all. You are all equal in every way. It is the differences in your belief systems that have created divisions so deep they have wiped out entire civilizations. The true word of God lies within each and every one of you. You are the truth. Do not look for it elsewhere.

Remember your potentiality as Divine beings to shift your awareness. Remember who you are and do not give your power to institutions who preach to you their doctrines to keep you in their control. This is not why you came here. You came here to create, not to be suppressed and disabled into thinking and believing you are "less than." Fully embrace the power that you are and create wonders for yourselves and your planet.

Love is All That Is. Remember who you are. You are the very essence of pure love—of the Divinity within you.

Change your minds to change your behaviors to bring your-selves new outcomes. Cultural and religious belief systems have kept you hostage from experiencing this. Live in the truth of who you are. Gather one another in this love and feel the Divinity that you are. Collective energy can move mountains. Realize your potentiality. The time is now.

It is time to awaken to the truth of All That Is. It is time to embrace this shift in your consciousness that is being poured onto you now, for this is the time to fully understand the truth of your creations and the need for the transference of energy toward collective manifestation through the energy of love and compassion.

We are here to assist you and to guide you.

Too much emphasis has been placed on what it is that you do not want and not enough on the love that is in the creation of what you do want. Take responsibility in knowing that you can begin to alter this mindset, for it is in your power to do so. You are focusing on the lack and not on the abundance of your creations, for there is plenty. As a global consciousness, you can bring in more of this abundance, fully realizing your great potentiality. The time is now.

Excuses will permeate throughout your consciousness, which will attempt to hold you to the comfort of where you are at this time. Great effort, great focus, and intention will bring you out of this false paradigm into full manifestation of the oneness that you all are—the oneness of pure infinite Source energy and love.

You are a part of the creation that brought you here. You are one with God, and you are here to create, not to settle in to what is commonly put forth to you by others.

Cultural and family belief systems are plaguing you. You are breathing in the constant replay that has come forth throughout your lifetimes. These are disempowering you. This is not who you are.

Break free from these limiting beliefs. Break free from all the rules and stipulations that are holding you from experiencing your ultimate potentiality. Love is who you are. Release the conditioned patterning of your minds of who you are not. Release the shame and the guilt. This is not who you are.

Love has no boundaries. You are love and you are loved. Change your minds to set yourselves free.

Your mind has influenced you into believing you are not enough, that you are flawed and undeserving. This is not who you are. You are not these limitations. You are not your mind. You are much greater.

Change your minds. Focus on the abundance and the potentiality of the Divine nature in you and change your minds for new beginnings to filter into your realities. You are the greatest creators. No one can be you and do this for you. You are here to feel and to be in allowance for spirit to work through you to assist you in lifting all the heaviness from your hearts.

Access and activate the highest magnificence of who you are. It is time to change your mindsets to create the life that you really wish for.

Be prepared to be faced with fear, for this is all your species knows. You are plagued with fear, for this is who you are at this time. This is what you are experiencing, for this is what you are constantly creating. You are manifesting fear-based outcomes, and these are inhibiting your growth.

You are making decisions that only create more dysfunction and more chaos and more destruction. Fear causes turmoil. Fear is not love. Fear is the opposite. This is not who you are.

Creating out of fear has not served you. It has put you in a place of isolation and defense, creating deep divisions amongst you, from personal to global.

Love your planet. Love your life. Love who you are. It is you who can transform everything. Do not give your power to the few, to those who care not about humanity but only about themselves. It is you who can create this shift in consciousness and awaken to the grandest light of who you are. The power is within you.

Create out of love, not out of fear. Alter the direction of your thinking.

Cultural biases only create separation. Respect one another with your differences and create together to awaken to the truth of your existence. The time is now to heal yourselves and heal your planet, for it is humanity who has put it where it is today.

Your planet is in dire need of love, unity, and peace. The vibration it is feeding from has brought it to the unbalanced state that it is. It is crying out for help. It is crying out for change. Change your minds to help your planet to change your reality.

Your old belief systems disable you from creating and experiencing fully and completely. The time is now to come to new understandings.

Believe and trust that you are the ultimate creators. This is your purpose. It is your choice to reposition your focus to assist in the planetary shift that is happening at this time. Change your minds to redirect the energy that has been creating the demise of your species and your planet.

Humanity has lost its way. Your planet is decaying. Awaken to this truth and accept responsibility to collectively bring forth a movement for transformation.

Place your intention on the creation of your choice. Create to experience the joy of life.

The time is now to recognize that it is you who can improve your lives and your world. Do not sit waiting for others to do the work for you. Do not sit in a state of despair. There is hope. There is hope when you see yourselves as oneness and work together. It all starts with you.

Your governments have not served you. Your governments have separated you. They are in compliance with power and greed. They have created division and competition. They care not for the collective.

Your governments have indeed not served you. Being in judgment does not serve you either. Do not take on the victim role. You are not victims. Taking on this perspective creates fear, which you are not. Do not give up your power. Actively create from a place of love, taking full responsibility for that which is before you at this time. Begin wherever it is that you are, and know that this is where you need to be.

You are not divided as you have been led to believe. Withdraw from following those who have fallen asleep. Follow your hearts. Follow the intention of unity and love to create the change that your soul so desires and needs.

It is in your power to bring forth new realities, and you can do this one step at a time. Think before you act. Feel before you act, and do what feels right. Do not be shamed into following others. Take the time to feel, to come into new understandings. The time is now to take your power and use it.

Awaken to your truth. You are fully capable of creating the abundance that you are ... the life that you so deserve.

Do not believe yourselves to be victims. There are no victims.

Let us clarify.

Believing this is an illusion. It is believing that you have no power or control over the situations you are experiencing. It is believing you are powerless.

This is not the truth. The reality is that you always have free will and choice, which puts you into full gear of empowerment. You can choose differently. No one is holding you back but yourselves.

Victimhood is believing you are less than. It is surrendering your power as soul creator. It is a limitation of the mind.

Take back your power. Break free from what it is that you do not want. This comes from not knowing what you do want. Your species tends to be in a state of confusion.

The victimhood perspective is a total surrender of your God-given power to execute your purpose in human form. Think again. The choice is yours.

There are no victims but the mind games that you are playing with yourselves. This place of non-existence has not and will not serve your higher purpose. It will keep you from experiencing your true selves ... the essence of purity that you are.

You are great creators of the universe. It is you who have the power to control all situations, all aspects of your lives, from relationships to manifestations of earthly disasters.

It is in your power to change how you are living. It is in your power to make the changes you all tend to complain about. Do not sit and wait for others to do this for you. Every one of you has the power to make a difference when you stand together in unity and love. You will create such a disturbance that inevitable transformation shall prevail. All obstruction shall diminish. You are the power that will transform it all.

A shift is in motion. The transformation process has already begun for many of you. Hold your intention to start your own movement. You are not alone. You are surrounded by angels, waiting to assist you. Feel this deeply to access it. Be open to it. Welcome it ... and ask.

Negative thinking patterns are limitations of your mind. Release them by changing your minds about them. It is that simple. Come to the realization that this is not you. You are greatness.

Your species has created misfortune with your mindsets as they are at this time. You are functioning at a very low vibrational state. You are in kindergarten in your earth school. The time has come to wake up and create differently.

Look deep within, for you have the ultimate power to manifest new and wonderful beginnings. This is what you need to awaken to. No one else can do this for you. One at a time, your energetic fields will merge and blend with others, and together create a solid force that will bring forth more bountiful outcomes. One at a time, you will join with others to create a powerful unified field of consciousness.

Be the change and begin by altering your attitudes. Understand fully that you can create a movement towards change. You can actively participate in the transformative process of your planet. Do not rely on others to do this for you.

Embrace this concept fully, for without each and every one of you, the power to shift and move your reality into a more positive direction will take longer and be more strenuous. Your planet is dying and so are you.

Throughout history, man has used his knowledge and expertise as a form of survival—survival of the fittest. Nothing has changed. Humanity has continued to sacrifice in order to succeed and bring down whomever and whatever comes in its way. This is the mindset of a five-year-old. You have shunned what you do not understand and belittled those sent to you to show you the way.

You have forgotten who you really are.

Throughout history, your species has separated itself not only from God but from yourselves, and from all who differ from you, for fear of loss. You have been violent. You have caused wars. This is all you have known. Your species has lived in fear and has created from this place of darkness.

Fear is what is poisoning your every part of you. It is paralyzing your ability to think clearly and to act with a loving heart. Through this state, you can only create more of the same ... more chaos and destruction. This is not who you are.

From this point forward, it is in your power to alter your reality. Begin by taking responsibility and raising your awareness to what is before you. Fully grasp the concept of unity and put aside the mundane attitudes of corruption and competition amongst you. Look at each other in wonder and amazement. You have been created of equal substance.

Allow love into your hearts. From a compassionate heart, you will find your answers. Love brings unity, which brings clarity and peace. This is who you are. This is what you are longing for ... all of you.

Make yourselves available for what is most important. Go within. You will find your answers. Take this time to raise your awareness and awaken to new possibilities. Creativity will flow, shifting your consciousness to new heights. Bring yourselves out of this delusional state of suffering.

Join forces with those who have already awakened. Be in the company of those who have compassion and love in their hearts—those who understand the unity of existence. Allow your consciousness to begin to shift to new directions. Take the time to stop and think. Take the time to pause from your busy lifestyles and your distractions, to fully embrace the longingness in your hearts for the peace and tranquility that you are made of.

Remember why you came here, as this is the biggest realization. You are Godly beings of creation and self-expression. You are here to manifest realities that will bring you to new heights of awareness. You are here to evolve. This is why you are here on planet earth: to evolve through your experiences. It is only in physicality that you may utilize your gift of creation. Once you pass, you are in different form. Evolution continues but in a different way.

Let us clarify.

The evolutionary process is a simple one. Once you transition into your next life, into the life of non-physical realities, the evolutionary process (although still in continuance) no longer holds the glory of physical manifestation. In the higher realms of existence, you evolve through service, assisting those either in physical or non-physical form.

Thus, it is now that you may feel and create to experience and evolve to higher ground—higher levels of consciousness that will bring forth new understandings and new, more-elevated insight in the actual truth of who you are. It is your time to unite with compassion and love for each other. It is your time to collectively create the world you wish to live in.

Your time is now. Your species is suffering, and so is your home. It is your God-given right to be in compliance with what is rightfully yours. Take it. This is your time. The time is now.

Bring yourselves back to the remembrance of your grand potentiality.

The time is now to remember that you are the greatest, most powerful creators. You can change your realities very, very quickly upon coming together, and co-creating in unison. Remember this truth. It is in your power and in your control to do what you wish with yourselves and with your planet.

Understand that much will be stirred and shifted in the process of restoration and stabilization.

Inevitable chaos, unrest, disease, and disharmony will persist. There will be tsunamis, earthquakes, volcanic eruptions, forest fires, flooding, scorching temperatures, ice storms, and destructive rainfalls. This is inevitable in your future, for this is what your species has created. Such imbalance will take major cleansing and clearing.

All that you have been given to sustain you is perishing ... every plant, insect, bird, every species, fish, sea mammal, wild and domestic animal. All are suffering. All are feeling this imbalance.

Your species has disturbed the natural order of life. You have poisoned your oceans, your streams, rivers, and lakes. You have poisoned your crops with GMOs, pesticides, and herbicides. You have poisoned your animals by inflicting them with pain and suffering, forcefully feeding them, and injecting them with poisons.

And many are wondering why you are getting sick.

You will experience great catastrophes. This is inevitable. Major cleansing is in dire need.

Wake up, people. Wake up to the reality of your creations. Begin now to move your reality in a more positive direction. The time is now.

Release what does not serve you. Withdraw from participation and communication with that which causes you grief, pain, and sorrow. Be in the company of those who have love in their hearts, for it is from this place that transformation will begin to unfold— your personal inner transformation.

Step away from those who continue to hurt you, those who function and exist from drawing the life-force energy from you, those who revolve around the unpleasantness of their own creations. Lovingly part ways.

Love who you are and who you are becoming, and only then may you begin to breathe in the essence of love: that which you truly are. You are the ultimate potentiality. This is who you are.

Withdraw from following those who have fallen asleep. Wake up and begin the transformation that will foster change. Take a stand. Voice your concerns. Do not sit back and allow your power to be taken. Speak your truths. Understand who you are and move forward with faith and with trust that you are supported by a greater power. You are greatly supported. More and more, you will realize and understand the essence of what we are speaking.

A great shift in consciousness is underway on your planet. The time is now to fully grasp this concept and move forward without fear.

You will be judged. You will be criticized. Without doubt, you will be ridiculed by those who fear the unknown, those who foster and feed on the delusion of separation, those who do not wish to join forces for fear of losing their external pleasures.

There will be many who will be shaking in fear.

One at a time, change your minds to awaken to new possibilities. Flow love to humanity.

One at a time, more and more will join in this movement and collectively bring about peaceful resolutions to create a shift towards solidarity and transformation.

Together you will build a new tomorrow for yourselves, your children, and your grandchildren. It is in your power, and it is rightfully yours to create.

Begin now. Understand fully the need to act now.

Make it your priority to take the time in each day to go within, to connect with your inner truth, to do what you need to do, to create the shift within you. Heal yourselves and your planet. The time is now.

More and more, your species will experience the destruction that you have created. More and more, you will come to an understanding that it is indeed your responsibility to assist in bringing back the balance necessary to restore your planet, for without her, you are nothing. You will no longer exist.

Stop poisoning your home.

Hatred contracts, diminishes, destroys
Suffering persists in suffocating its people
Fear

Rising consciousness transforming
Transcending into power
Love

4
You Have Been Lied To

As resilient as your planet is, resilience is not the issue. The issue is decay. Your planet is decaying little by little. The glory of what surrounds you will no longer serve you.

Come to this understanding and be the creators that you are meant to be. Create with full awareness, and you will not be disappointed.

We urge you to remember and take the steps needed to begin the process of your personal transformation.

The time is now to slow down and take the time to digest what is happening in your planet. The time is now to understand more completely, to begin your process of self-development.

Take the time to awaken to the truth of what you have collectively created. The time is now to reflect and move forward.

Clarity will surface with the realization of the oneness that you are. You are not separate in and of each other.

An information highway propels itself into networking with the vibrations of life. Without this network, you are nothing. You are in a grid-system highway, co-existing and vibrating simultaneously with all around you. Your energetic fields are passing through and merging with others co-existing and co-creating at multi-level frequencies.

Nothing else matters but the matter that you are putting forth each and every moment. Particles of matter blend with others, and this is how you function. You are not on your own. You are all interconnected through an information highway and grid system.

Everything co-exists and co-creates with you. Everything is matter. All living and non-living things contain matter. You are all one big ball of energy. This is what you are in simple terms.

You are God's creations, and God is one. You are an extension of Source energy.

Breaking your existence down to this micro-organism will bring you to the understanding that you are all made of the same. There is no one better than the other. With this remembrance, you will have the flexibility necessary to absorb what has been put before you.

The concept of unity must be understood and accepted to move forward. More and more are awakening to this truth. More and more are shifting, elevating their consciousness, opening up to new insights, to new possibilities.

Your species is undergoing a process—a process of self-discovery, a process of growth and expansion. You are being supported by a much greater power on this journey. You are being given the tools that will assist you as you continue on this path. Slowly, you will come to new understandings that will foster your growth. Slowly, you will embrace new beginnings that will bring you out of the suffering state that plagues your planet.

There is no need to live in fear. Love is the highest vibration. Be the love that you are meant to be. Remember that you are purity of love and joy.

There is no need to live within the limitations of your minds. Break free. We will show you the way to end all your sorrow.

There is no need to focus on others. There is no need to worry. Focus only on yourselves. All will unfold naturally for each and every one of you.

More and more will join forces until there are so many that those who are in continual resistance will inevitably remember. The energetic level will be vibrating at a force so high that it will shake them out of their forgetfulness.

Remember the essence of who you are.

Practice mindful awareness. Understand that what you are experiencing at each moment of your moments is the actual reality of what is. Focus to bring yourselves to the truth that nothing else really matters because nothing else really exists.

The beauty of each moment is what is real. All of life moves in a frequency that is so vast and so transient that there cannot be any other moment that is identical to the previous. What you are experiencing is what is real.

Stop dwelling on what is not real. Stop dwelling on your past. Stop dwelling on what may not be in your future. You are creating anxiety within you. You are making yourselves sick.

It is the present moment that holds the power to change everything. It is your state of mind at each of your moments. It is your awareness. Focus on the power of your moments to move your lives and your planet into a more loving state.

You have been given all that you need to live an abundant life—all of you. Your planet is equipped to completely sustain you. Every corner of your earth is filled with ample resources. There is enough for all. You lack nothing.

You have been led to believe resources are limited, that there is not enough to provide for you. This belief is reinforcing the limitations that you believe you are. When you continue in this state, there will never be enough. This is what you are attracting.

Many of your people are living in poverty. They have adopted the victimhood perspective. They believe there is not enough, and thus continue to bring this into their experiences. They are suffering in the global energy of dysfunction.

Bring yourselves to the understanding that you have been mislead. Do not accept what others are presenting to you. Think for yourselves to come to the understanding that your world is complete and has always been. There is abundance for all. Resources are many, and they are available.

Assist your people in lifting themselves out of their suffering states. Raise the energy of your planet to release the suffering of so many who believe that there is no other way. There is another way. You have merely not accessed it. We are here to remind you.

Those who seek to advance themselves and only themselves, with disregard for the collective, have overpowered you. Your species has allowed this. You live your lives unconsciously. You have allowed yourselves to be manipulated in so many ways by those who care only for themselves, those who believe they are superior—those who have completely lost themselves in the delusion of who they are not.

Bring yourselves to the understanding that you are all one. You are the collective. Understand that you need to take charge of your lives. Stop entrusting others with it.

Corporations have taken over your agricultural industries. These are not in compliance with the natural order of life. They have no love for humanity. Self interest is what drives them. They have introduced methodologies to convince you of the need to modify produce to support the belief in the lack that defines you. This is not the truth. There is abundance for all.

They have stripped you of the right to consume products in their most natural states. They have stripped the nutrients from your soils and have poisoned your environments.

Their ways have not provided solutions to your global dysfunction. Their ways have further impaired the dysfunction that already exists.

Awaken to this truth. Nothing has changed. These corporations are destroying the purity of who you are, offering you what does not support you, locking you into a suppressed, depressed state whereby disease floods your core existence. Their mission is to keep you under their control.

Wake up people.

You are consuming sick produce. This is siphoning the energetic balance out of you, stifling you from being the creative thinkers and creators that you are.

Do not continue to be so trusting. Trust what you know from deep within you. Listen to your voice within. Bring yourselves back into alignment.

You have been led to believe there is not enough. This is one of the greatest misconceptions on your planet at this time.

The poor are getting poorer. They are dying of starvation. There is no need.

Wake up, people. Stop supporting this insanity. Take charge of your lives. You have one life to live. Live it fully in abundance, with peace and harmony. We know this is what you want. You can have it.

Raise your awareness and stand your ground. Voice your concerns now. Take charge by your own willingness to alter your reality. Be the change you wish to see in your world—well stated by Mahatma Gandhi.

You are beginning to understand more of what is happening in your world. You are beginning to understand that what you are consuming is killing you. We are pleased that so many of you are beginning to see the light.

Take charge by your own willingness to change your lives. Refrain from purchasing products that have been tampered with, genetically modified into something they are not, falsified, and poisoned with toxicity that is blocking your creativity.

Feed your body healthier alternatives to assist in bringing back the balance that you need. Cleanse and clear yourselves of toxins. Create a healthier you. Choose wisely.

You have been lied to, and you have been cheated from the natural resources of your environment. You are being controlled and suppressed. Interest lies in increasing profit, not in helping humanity. They care not about your survival. They care not that they are contributing in making you sick. They care not they are killing you.

They believe that they are separate from you. This is a false belief. They have lost their way.

Wake up to your reality. The time is now. Wake up and take a stand on changing your future, changing your lives to save yourselves and heal your world. The time is now.

Love who you are. Feed your body clean and natural products. Consume products that are in their most natural forms. Withdraw from consuming chemicals and ingredients that you cannot pronounce. Here are the hidden dangers. Make wiser, more mindful decisions.

Purchase local products that are from farmers who have love in their hearts, as these are the products that will assist in raising your vibration and support you.

Support your farmers. They are doing their best, trying to sustain suitability for the natural state of their products.

Consume raw, natural products that come from areas that are close to you. Whatever is shipped to you will not serve you. They are void of nutrients—void of love. They are not cared for. They are mass produced for mass consumption, with disregard for nutritional value to the consumer. They are meant to fill your bellies and provide temporary satisfaction. They are meant to fill the pockets of corporations with financial abundance, making the rich richer and the poor poorer and sicker. Realize this truth to make better choices.

Consume organic produce. The more you do this, the greater the assistance that you will receive. The financial ease that you are looking for will come to you. Be in alignment with what will serve you. Do not be so afraid. You will come to new understandings that will foster your growth and allow you the flexibility to purchase what you need to enhance your development.

The vibration of food has not been understood fully. Understand all is energy. What you are feeding your bodies must be taken more seriously.

Grow your own whenever possible. Love is the highest vibration. This is what will enhance your natural intuitive state: products that have been lovingly cared for.

Bless your food. Raise its vibration from wherever it has come. Cleanse and purify negativity that has been infused in it from all handling it from start to finish. Understand all is energy and all gets translated into the product's energetic field. Bless it and bless those who helped to bring it to your table. Assist in releasing all that doesn't serve you. Think before you eat. Have love in your hearts.

Your awareness and intention will awaken you to new possibilities. You will come to new understandings one step at a time. Awaken to this truth.

You are poisoning your bodies and your minds by consuming what lacks the energy of love. It is affecting every aspect of your beingness. What you are consuming is suppressing your personal growth at all levels—physical, mental, emotional, and spiritual. The time is now to make more conscious choices.

Come to an agreement within yourselves to alter your reality. Recognize the need for transformation. Believe in yourselves as the creators that you are, and take a stand to change your lives.

Take charge of your lives, as you can make a difference one at a time, collectively joining forces, loving yourselves, and taking better care of yourselves.

Your species tends to go through the motions of each day without much awareness. You operate robotically. You follow your routines. You work, eat in haste, and work again. You busy yourselves. Distraction is what you know and live by.

You do not sleep well. You do not eat well. You do not communicate well, nor understand and enjoy your present moments.

Realize you are not robots. You are creative beings who have incarnated to create your lives by your design. Use your gifts.

Wake up people. The time is now to slow down, recognize this truth and be the conscious creators that you are meant to be. The time is now to awaken from your trance states.

Wake up, access, and activate what is rightfully yours.

Your species has created the concept of time. This restricts the natural flow of creativity. You have limited yourselves, contracting your flow to the limitation of time. This has restricted you from living in your truth, and from having the freedom to create more fully.

Let us clarify.

There is no time limitation. There is only the moment you are experiencing. This is the time. There is no other real time. What you have inputted is time restrictions to manage your days. This has ultimately created stressful realities, since you are always in need of more time. You are racing with time. Your species lives with frustration. You live with anxiety. You have put limitations on yourselves. There is no need.

Breaking up your day into time constrictions has not served you. Know that you have more time than you need. There is much abundance of all that you need in your lifetimes, including time. Be more aware of your moments, and you will recognize this truth. When you are living fully in your moments, immersed in the truth of who you are, when you are living your lives with joy, you will recognize this truth.

Managing without this concept will revitalize humanity. This is your future. Your future needs restructuring, and this will be the first concept that will be addressed.

The time is now to raise your awareness and begin your own personal process of growth and development.

Realize that it is within you to manage your lives the way you wish. You are in complete control of what you are experiencing. You are in complete control of what you are choosing to experience, at this time.

You have brought these to your realities, whatever they may be, the good and the bad, the happy and the sad. You have brought them to assist you in your evolution.

Your future is in your control, as is your present. Be mindful and remember this truth. Trust in yourselves, and in the power that you have, to make your lives what you want them to be.

Remember that you are the greatest creators. Remember that you have the power to manage your lives free of time restrictions. Remember the truth of who you are and the great potentiality of your existence. This will give you the courage to return to the authentic simplicity of who you are. From this place, clarity will follow.

Mindfulness shall prevail—the understanding that you are not alone. You are well supported from Source, from the God of your choosing, whatever you wish to call the greatest intelligence.

Together, one by one, you will remember and help each other in your awakening process. Together, you will create better realities that will enhance your existence. Your choices will come from a place of clarity of what will serve you as a community—as one community working in unison. Your choices will be of higher value, as you will be functioning at a higher vibrational frequency.

Remember that you are not separate. Remember that your planet needs assistance. Remember that your species is dwindling. Remember that your species has lost its way. You need to be in this remembrance.

Slow yourselves down to your remembrance. Take the time in each day to be with yourselves, to be in this remembrance. Go within to be in the stillness of who you truly are. You are the peace that lies within. You are the love that resides within. It is time to live in this truth—to live in this remembrance.

Many are suffering. Many of your species are void of the essence of the purity of who you are.

You are of the essence of God. The time is now to reclaim it, to return yourselves to your true selves. From this place of remembrance, you can create the beauty of who you are. You can create the life that is rightfully yours. You can become the greatest that you have ever been, functioning at the optimum potentiality of your existence. Create this life for yourselves, which will enhance your soul and allow you the flexibility to manage your lives effectively, with love, within the balance of all creations.

Create the existence of your choosing with love and compassion. Work together. Help one another. One step at a time, more and more will gain greater insight. Alter your reality to live to your highest potentiality, for it is within you to experience. The time is now. Change your minds. The time is now to open your minds to see things differently.

The concept of money is another culprit of your existence. It has not supported you. It is contributing to your downfall.

There is competition amongst you which has created evil within you and around you. Your species is not living with the energy of the highest vibration. There is an innate need for accumulation ... a hunger for materialism. You desire power, and you live divided.

There is no one better and more deserving than the other. Understand this fully.

The more your species has the more you want. There is no inner growth in this reality. There is greed and suffering. There is self-righteous behavior. There is manipulation and self-centeredness. There is separation.

Your world needs major restructuring to bring it back to the balance of who you are within the cosmos of your existence. Your planet is in decay. Your species is destroying itself. Wake up. You have fallen asleep.

The time is now to contemplate and understand deeply. The power is within you to take charge of your realities and transform them. Create a shift. It is awaiting you. There is hope.

You have forgotten that what you do to each other you do to yourselves. You are hurting each other. You are hurting yourselves, for this is the law of the universe. Whatever it is that you put forth will come back to you even greater, for you are oneness. Be more mindful, for this is the truth.

You are not separate from one other. Allow this to resonate deep within your consciousness to begin the much-needed process of transformation. Recognize this truth as the biggest truth of all. You are not separate. You are interconnected. You are one unified field of consciousness, fed by Source energy. You are Source energy beings.

We are planting the seeds of higher consciousness into many of you who are holding the intention for self-growth. More and more will open themselves to new understandings recognizing the need for change, recognizing the truth of life ... of God.

Your tomorrows will be much brighter as this movement spreads throughout your planet. Love, compassion, and peace will permeate.

The time is now. The time is now to start your personal process, to bring forth the light that is glowing within you and spread it to the darkest places on your planet. Believe that you can make a difference. You are the most powerful creators. It is within you to assist in the transformative process of your evolution.

Accept this power. Take responsibility and create the shift that will enhance you. This will place you in a higher frequency that will allow you to spread this powerful vibration amongst you. The time is now to activate the light in you.

Release your fears. This is not who you are. Access what is rightfully yours by opening to your higher power. Release your doubts and know in your hearts that you are in physicality to live to your fullest potential, happy and at peace with yourselves and with others. You are not here to suffer. You are not stuck in your realities, unless you choose to be.

Choose differently. Raise yourselves up to who you truly are. The choice is yours, and the choice is put before you to assist you in your awakening.

Violence amongst you is increasing daily. Hatred fosters your existence, not love. Look around and you will notice your dysfunction. Slow down and take notice.

Many go through the motions of each day in haste, in distraction of what is real. You are alive. Celebrate this truth. You are breathing in the beauty of life. Celebrate.

Many are withdrawn from the joy of living.

You are equipped to manifest your deepest desires. You are equipped to bring forth your most glorious realities—the realities of your choosing. This is in your power to do so.

Awaken to this truth and open yourselves up to newer possibilities. The time is now to stop sabotaging the life that you are meant to live.

Your species is living in a state of immense sleepiness. Dense fog permeates from deep within. You tend to blame, challenge, and neglect yourselves. You have trouble with forgiveness.

Your species is self-righteous and self-absorbed. You are not living in your truth. You are living in a low vibrational state, and the energies around you are supporting this negativity.

Alter the vibration you are emanating to experience the love and light that you truly are.

Invite loving relationships into your experiences. Remove those that no longer serve you. Bless them and release them, for they were placed before you to teach you what you needed to learn, to show you what you needed to see. Bless them, for they have assisted in your evolution.

Have no resistance to what unfolds before you. Trust and go with the flow of life with no resistance. Allow God to lead you—to show you the way. Your higher self will take care of you. It will show you the way when you allow it.

Honor yourselves as the loving, compassionate beings that you are and do what is necessary to begin to experience this. The time is now to take charge and make the changes necessary to begin your personal process of development.

Years gone by
In pain and sorrow
Holding back,
withdrawing tomorrows

Years gone by
Suffering greatly
In silence and sadness
Beholding little

Years gone by
In fear and desperation
Life passing by

Judgment and bewilderment
A part of this world, far removed
Loneliness unbearable

Who am I?
In search and in wonder
I find myself

5
You Are Light Co-Creators

As soul creators, you are all on different paths with different experiences to foster your growth. You are all at different places. Some of you are living in your truths and are assisting others on their paths, while others are struggling to find their way, living a life of victimhood with blame and shame and deeply rooted anger.

Begin wherever you are now. Begin your own inner transformation.

What one will do is not what the other may do at this time. You are all on different paths, and you all need to understand this.

You can evolve from wherever it is that you are. Understanding this concept is vital in moving forward. Help yourselves and start from wherever you are. Want it to achieve it. Your intention must be clear, without doubt, and without fear. You are well supported by a higher intelligence. Understand this.

Access your power. Create a shift by moving yourselves out of your undesirable states. Do what feels right. Feel your way into a different direction with gratitude and love in your hearts. Find yourselves once again by grasping the light within you. See and feel the blessings that you have, for only then may you open yourselves to more.

We know it is hard to see yourselves as conscious creators, when many of you are in your dormancy states. It is difficult to admit that you have consciously created what you are now experiencing, within your own little circle and within the entire cosmology of your existence. It is a bitter reality that your species has contributed to your demise, both consciously and unconsciously.

Understand that your planet is in absolute need of assistance, and so are you. Recognize that you have the power to create change. The power is within you.

Take the time to go within. Take the time to slow yourselves down. Open your eyes and open your minds in order to recognize the importance of much-needed change.

There is hatred amongst you. There is division. There is little tolerance—little acceptance of one another.

Respect the differences that you all have and recognize that you are all made of the same. You are all a part of the great Source of All That Is. Develop a compassionate heart and accept those around you. Accept yourselves.

The violence, the injustice, the greed, and the upheaval that is permeating now has resulted with this notion you are separate.

Your countries have separated you. Your governments have separated you. Your religions have separated you. Your cultures have separated you. Your colour has separated you. Your past has separated you. Your beliefs have separated you. This is the biggest separation. You are lost.

One faith does not differ from the other. All faiths come from the same place: God. There is only one. Your species has misinterpreted the teachings of your holy books. It is humanity that has divided you. There is no one way to God. There are many. There is no right or wrong way. It is all in your perception.

Do not judge. Do not criticize and believe that you know more than others. Follow your heart. Follow what is pulling you and know this is your right way. There are many roads to Heaven. There are many roads to the realization of the self.

Those who harm, sacrifice, and pledge allegiance to their gods have fallen asleep. They have been trained in hatred. They live in the truth of their leaders, who foster separation. These leaders manipulate and mislead to serve their own purposes. They fear the loss of control and power.

This is not the true word of God. This is not what God wants. God wants or needs nothing. God is everlasting peace, which belongs to you. That's what God is.

God is pure love and light, compassion and free will. God loves you all and has gifted you with choice. Make your life what you want it to be. Every decision that you make is by your free will. Be more conscious of your decisions. Ask for guidance. Ask for the light of the Divine to flow through you for your highest good. You will not be disappointed.

God loves you deeply, sending you heightened awareness, assisting you by helping you to be open to new concepts and new ideas that will foster new beginnings. You are not limited as you may think. You are infinite beings of creation, and you are offered support of the highest caliber.

Forgive yourselves and forgive all who have hurt you, all whom you believe to have harmed you. Accelerate your process of self-discovery. Forgive with an open heart to allow love energy to penetrate and permeate your entire beingness.

Love all those who cross you and bless them, for everyone has their own understandings. Be the change. Be the love to raise the vibration of your planet to heal itself. Be what you wish to see in your world, and you will attract it. Be the love that dwells deep inside. Bring it out and share it. You are oneness with All That Is. You are oneness with life.

Love openly without judgment, for this is within you. Love shall take you to heightened awareness on a journey toward the elevation of your consciousness. Peaceful resolution to your challenges may then be awoken. Clarity will facilitate the evolution of your species. Begin this process now.

You are pure light beings, and you are on this planet, in form, to experience. You are in physical form for this purpose. You are here to experience and to evolve through your experiences.

Remove yourselves from the stagnant energies that you have created. You are not stuck in your realities as you may believe. As conscious creators, you may move forward and upward if you so desire. You may move into higher dimensions, higher levels of consciousness, whereby you may open to new seeds of growth and lovingly embrace the magical beauty of who you are. Consciously choose differently, to experience differently.

Your species has been living unconsciously, which has created chaos and dysfunction. Be more mindful and be the creators that God has made you to be. Remove yourselves from the limitations of your minds. You are not your mind. You are much greater.

Love will lead the way. Love will open your hearts to forgiveness. Love will cleanse and heal your past hurts. Love is All That Is. Remember this very truth.

Channel your life-force energy to access your truth. Raise your vibrations to assist in altering your egoic, catastrophic selves. Put aside your egos to move forward. Your species is killing each other with your thoughts, your words, and your actions. Everything is vibrating, co-existing and co-creating. Everything is energy. The vibrational frequency of your planet is affecting you. This is what you have created.

Ask for Divine assistance. It is there.

There is an abundance of assistance available to you, both in physical and non-physical form. Understand you are well supported, never forgotten.

The choice is yours to shift your focus—to align yourselves with the beauty that lies within. Access this truth to experience it. You are Divine beings.

The sooner you come to accept this, the sooner you may rejoice in the manifestation of your true desires. Understand you hold the power to make your lives what you want them to be. Accept who you are to empower yourselves.

Raise your vibration to raise the vibrational frequency of your planet. You are one. You are one energy field of consciousness, vibrating simultaneously, affecting each other and your world.

More and more of you want to understand yourselves and who you are in relation to all. More and more are opening to the wisdom of who you are. This is the truth.

More and more want to improve your lives and make a difference for the collective. This is the wonderful truth. We are pleased that more and more are in this understanding and are holding this intention.

The ascension process has begun.

Many of you are shedding layers upon layers of the old you, coming into greater understandings.

Many of you are awakening to the light and love of who you are. You are living your lives with purpose, living without judgment, fearlessly moving forward learning more and more along your path, living in the peace and harmony of that which you are made of. We encourage you to live in this truth. Live fully.

Accept where you are completely and know that you are where you need to be. This will put you in allowance for newfound inspiration. Do not hold true to what you were, what you did, what you could have done, what you said, what you could have said—how you wish things were different. Do not live with regret, worry, and stress. You are where you need to be, with the understanding that you can begin from wherever you are at this time. Make the choice to start your new day—to start your new beginnings.

You are given opportunities to move forward—on-going opportunities that will enable you to make better choices. Allow yourselves the freedom to begin fresh, new, and clean, clear of old beliefs, clear of past judgments and prejudices, clear of wrongdoings, for these are all here presenting themselves to you to enable you the opportunity for growth and expansion.

Begin new beginnings fresh from this vantage point: new beginnings of altered thinking. Believe that you are infinite, for this is your truth. You are Divinity expressing itself.

As sovereign beings, you can alter your reality at any given moment by choosing differently.

We love you and we want you to believe in yourselves, in the power that you have, in the power that you are. Believe this to access it. You are not limited by any means. Listen to your hearts, not your logical, thinking minds that wish you to stay where you are, in the old habitual patterns, with belief systems that no longer serve you, belief systems that never served you, belief systems that keep you where you are now: separate from who you are in relation to the totality of life, separate from Source.

Know and understand that you are much greater. You are supreme beings. You are an expression of God itself. That's who you are. Believe this to access it.

The time is now to shift the density of your creations.

Lift yourselves up and create the reality that is of higher caliber—the reality that you are all wanting. Lead with your hearts, not with your minds.

Many of your species have already suffered disasters. Understand that it is in your power to change this.

Your planet is restructuring itself in order to maintain its balance, to sustain itself. It is within you to assist in this restructuring. Assist your home to lessen the impact that it will have on you as a species. Raise your personal vibration, to raise the vibration of the collective, to assist in the global transformation of your planet.

Acknowledge that there is a need. Become aware of what is happening around you. Take responsibility. Take ownership. Become more mindful of how you are living your lives.

These are the first steps.

Once you begin this process, you will not be disappointed. Trust in the process, for it is within you. This is a transformation process that involves all of humanity.

Many are working with you to assist you. There are councils of non-physical beings working with each of you.

This book has not come to you by chance. It is you who has chosen to be where you are now, ready for this information to unfold before you, ready to embark on new developments. It is you who has chosen to listen, to awaken to new wonderful possibilities. We are so very pleased.

Connect to Source, to the pure light of Divinity, to align with your own personal power. Raise your vibration to be in alignment with who you really are. Remove the distractions that come before you, which block the flow of your creative intelligence. Be in stillness. Go within. You will find what you are looking for.

Ask with an open heart, without fear or judgment. Love yourself enough to ask. Be fearless in moving forward, for only then may you bring to yourselves more and more insight and inspiration, which will assist you in your development. Allow the flow of Divine consciousness to enter through you and align you with your soul. Allow this flow to run smoothly, choosing and believing you are of this greatness.

Surrender the negative thought patterns that keep you from moving forward—that keep blocking the flow. Have faith and move forward.

Take responsibility. Do not place the pressures of your todays on others. This brings hostility, anger, and resentment.
Be with yourselves to honour who you are, to realize the potential that you have. Do not be in judgment.

The time is now to awaken, realize, and access the grand potential of who you are.

We know and we understand the difficulties that you are experiencing. We see the darkness that permeates your planet. The time is now to understand that it is in your hands to initiate and implement the inspiration and creativity that is being offered you.

We are here to assist you in raising your consciousness, one step at a time, one person at a time.

Open yourselves up to the potentiality of who you are. You are light co-creators. Together you can move forward and upward, elevating the consciousness of your planet and assisting everyone and everything—all of God's creations.

Begin by seeing the light in you. Believe that you are the greatness, the wonder, the magnificence of your creator.

Consciously choose the path you wish to follow. Choose to see clearly. Affirm the light that you are. This is your choice. From here, you may begin the choice of all creation, to be the stillness for clarity to permeate, for answers to come forth, for inspiration to fill your consciousness. Open your connection to Divinity, for you are a part of this. Open yourselves up to what is rightfully yours. Connect yourselves to Source. You have not been forgotten.

The time is now for humanity to awaken. Your species has forgotten the love and compassion that you are made of.

Slowly, more and more are beginning to see yourselves as soul creators, awakening to your truth, elevating your consciousness to the highest of high potentialities. You are opening to the truth of who you are, accessing and activating your power.

Love will permeate, for love is your truth. This is who you are. This is the magnificence of your creation.

Feel deeply. Be in stillness to feel. Trust in the unknowingness. With trust and with confidence, fearlessly move forward. The time is now to change your lives to make life work for you, not against you. Begin now to make the choice that will change your lives.

Consider all your resources. There are many available to you. Use these in a way to uplift you. Use what you already have, to support your higher need, together as one unit, one family.

Your species is losing itself in the magnetic pull of its choosing. Put aside your electronic devices. Release yourselves from the grasp of technology. Stop relying on the falsehoods of your creations. They are distracting you from living in the truth of who you are.

The time is now to awaken to the reality of your mindless creations. Without the morality behind your technology, there can never be love. Your technology is not supporting you. It is used to disempower you. This is the sad truth. The focus is on personal gain.

Technological development has furthered your existence well beyond its means. It has created madness. Humanity has lost its humanness. Without this, you are nothing.

Cloning is an example of this dysfunction. It is not a discovery that will foster your growth. It has made you into instruments of misguided fortune. Your species tends to believe this is your answer. You believe this is the answer to your evolution. You believe this will enhance your growth. You have sadly lost the meaning of life—what it is meant for.

It is this mindlessness that has led your species to where you are today. Have more awareness.

Along with the technological advancements come the medical advancements, which are vast and wonderful, however also lacking in humanness. These will not serve you. They will contribute to your downfall.

Use your advancements with mindfulness. Fill yourselves with optimism that with these discoveries you may serve in a bigger way, for you have the tools. Be mindful and use these tools to better yourselves and your future as a collective. Work together to see this happen. Work together, using all the gifts and talents that are offered you to uplift and empower you to enrich your lives.

Be mindful of your creations. Think independently. Do not follow the institutionalized thinking patterns of those who wish to satisfy their longing for more and more power and control. This self-righteous optimism of these leaders need not continue.

Act now, for this is the time. There is hope for a better tomorrow. Love will prevail, for this is who you are. Awaken to the truth of who you are.

Those with the greatest powers may destroy you with their advancements. They may wipe you away. It is in their power and in their control. They are consumed with gaining more and keeping you separate. This greed for power will destroy your masses.

The time is now to collectively shift the energy of your planet to assist in the awakening of your world leaders. Begin within. Begin by choosing to mindfully develop your inner growth. Choose to help yourselves, in order to help each other. You are one Divine family.

Bring back what is rightfully yours. Bring back your inner power and alter your reality. The time is now. Alter your thinking patterns, for you have the power to make this change. Bring back to yourselves who you really are.

Do not complain and criticize. This is the energy of fear. It will keep you from experiencing yourselves fully. You can change your world with the most powerful energy of all—love.

It is time to wake up and understand that your planet needs you. It is time to partake in this very important planetary restructuring.

Your planet is going through a major transition, and it needs your assistance to return to her natural state and restore the natural balance of all living things.

There will be natural disasters and many. There will be imbalance in the largest way. This is inevitable. Your planet is suffering and longing to return to its natural state.

Work together and bring your home back to balance. You are all in this together.

More and more will listen and will comply. More and more of you will understand. You are an extension of God. You are not separate. You have the power to alter whatever you wish. You are the greatest creators. Understand this fully.

Stop creating imbalance. Stop fostering hatred and separation. There is no need for fear. Fear creates more imbalance.

Look within to find your answers. Slow down and listen. Feel. Use your senses, and you will begin to understand so much more, for this is the language of the soul. Feel. Listen to your inner being-ness. Slow yourselves down long enough to begin to see the light in you. Your answers lie within. Use your senses, and you will be awakened.

Take the time to breathe. Really breathe in to fill your lungs. Feel the joy of life. Take the time to breathe deeply. Slow down. There is no need to continue to live without purpose. There is always enough time when you understand the value of mindful existence.

What you are experiencing in your own space is what you have created and co-created with others in your personal circle. What you are experiencing globally is what you have all created energetically, with your vibrations at an all-time low.

Trust and believe that you have chosen your reality—your experiences at this time ... all of it. You have brought them to you.

See them as the Divinity that they are, for with these experiences you are brought closer and closer to the light of who you are. It is through this darkness that light may enter. Learn and grow from your experiences. Choose to move forward.

Do not blame others. Do not put blame on circumstances, for you are the circumstances. You have chosen your paths, and you can choose differently. Move into more mindful, loving realities filled with joy, peace, and compassion ... that which you are.

Love is the driving force of unity. Love will bring you together. Love is All That Is. Love is the highest vibration of all.

All your negative emotions derive from fear, which is where your planet is, at this time. Fear is the driving force of your existence. It is fear that has created the monstrosities of your realities, the injustices, and the displeasures. You are not of this darkness.

You are of the light. You are of God, for you are an extension of the energy of pure Source. You and God are not separate. You are the light and the love of All That Is. You have merely forgotten.

We are here to remind you, to assist you in moving forward and upward into the next dimensional state, whereby there will be an opening of your hearts, an understanding of the unity of all in existence. Rejoice in the glory of the evolution of your consciousness.

The time is now to awaken to this truth. Remember this to come out of your darkness.

The time is now to rejoice in the beauty of who you are. You are the love and the light that shines within. The time is now to bring yourselves back to yourselves. Your world is crumbling. Your people are dying. You are killing yourselves. You are killing each other. What you do to others, you do to yourselves. What you are seeing is mirroring what you are creating. There is injustice of all kinds in your world.

World leaders with their lust for power and greed continue to overshadow your power. They suppress the beauty of who you are. You are not free to make your own choices when you are held captive by those in greater powers. You are not free, and you have chosen to allow this.

Management of your countries has fallen victim to the individualized thinking patterns of leaders whose desire is more power, more wealth, and more control. Your system of divisiveness of your nations is not working. You are dividing your home.

You are not divided. Wake up to this truth. You are not separate from each other, as you have made yourselves to be.

Rightfully take back what belongs to you. Take back your freedom and live in fulfillment of who you are, with love in your hearts. All will fall into place with love as your driving force. With this frequency, move forward, and you will not be disappointed. The time is now.

Take the time to think and understand where your species is with how you are functioning. Take the time to think. Be with yourselves to awaken to the truth.

Do not resist. Do not be in denial. Do not continue in this way, as this way will keep you isolated and in a suffering state. Your species will never be happy. You will never feel the joy of who you are. You will never feel the joy of life. You will experience the temporary pleasures of accumulation and superficial satisfaction.

Inevitably, one by one, you will come to the realization of the oneness of existence. There is hope and promise. You will all unite once again.

Begin in this place of wholeness, knowingly creating the abundant life that is yours. Be the truth that exists within. The time is now to bring it forward.

Your species is living in a primitive state of consciousness, whereby greed, corruption, and personal gain rule. This is not a very real state. It is not real in that it does not allow you the freedom of living with peace and love for one another. This is not what is real.

What is real is that you are all in this together. The sooner you realize this, the sooner you will be in alignment with your soul, which will allow you the freedom of full manifestation of all your desires. The choice is yours.

You are living in a state of lack and accumulation. You are living in a materialistic, individualized, competitive state, which is driving you further and further apart. This is not who you are. This is not why you came here.

Begin now to manifest who you really are. Return to the love that you are and the love that you have for one another.

In the silence of the night
Comes the burst of infinite possibilities
For it is at this time
Faith and trust renews itself

6
Choose Awareness

Who are you really?

Think more deeply about who you are to bring yourselves to the realization that you are more than you believe you are.

Are you the lawyers and the doctors, the homemakers and the teachers? Are you the farmers and the factory workers, the entrepreneurs and the engineers? Is this who you are? You may very well believe this is who you are, but are you really?

Are you the fathers and the mothers, the parents and the grandparents, the sisters and the brothers? Is this who you really are? Think again.

All of what you think you are is limiting you and keeping you in a locked, suppressed state, in a state of separation ... and this is all temporary.

Your species has consumed yourselves with the identity of what you do, but are you really what you do? Is this all you think you are, for this is living in the limitation of your mind.

You are the oneness, the totality of all. You are the unity by which all exists. See yourselves as this to alter your beliefs about you. All of what you so believe you are is keeping you from experiencing yourselves fully.

You are much more than your limiting beliefs. You have assumed these roles, and these are all temporary.

Do not identify yourselves with that which you are not. Do not keep yourselves separate. You are all equal substance. You have all come from the same. You are Divinity expressing itself fully. This is who you are.

Come to this awareness to bring in the love and compassion that is missing at the global level. Understand the unity of all in existence, and you will understand the need for change. Change your minds to change your realities.

Be in remembrance that Divine support is flowing to you. One step at a time, you will alter your reality and live in the truth of who you are, in the abundant life that is rightfully yours. Each of you will comply to the inevitable restructuring of your existence. More and more will understand and will assist in the ascension process.

Do not be so concerned with others. Be more focused with yourselves. Do the work that is needed to create within yourselves the peace that will bring you closer and closer to the simplicity of who you are. Manifest from this place of light and spread joy and love to all around you.

Do not be concerned with others. Be only concerned with yourselves. Do your part, and you will be rewarded greatly. Nothing else matters but you. This is where it all starts. Love yourselves as no other. Be the light in the darkness. Remember who you really are. It all starts with you.

Do not look elsewhere, waiting and expecting others to bring forth changes—changes in your governments, economies, educations, religions, or families. Do not wait for others to change their ways. Do your part in changing your world. It all starts with you. Be the change to experience it. Set your intentions and allow this powerful energy to enter and flow within you and around you. Set this in motion to experience it.

Mindful relaxation will get you there. Take the time to structure your days to incorporate this much needed and necessary time for yourselves. Join others and collectively assist one another. Go within and experience the stillness of your higher self. Begin each day with the understanding that you are not alone. You are never alone. You are well-supported by a much greater power.

Allow the beauty of who you are, and the interconnectedness that you are, within the matrix of all in existence, to shine through you.

Be in allowance for higher realms to assist you. Your Divine team is with you, supporting you, as they are an extension of you. They want what you want: peace and love to flow through you and to all. They love you and see you as an extension of who they are. The light in you shines as the light in them. For some, it shines brighter than others. You are at different places on your paths. You are all where you need to be, and you can begin from there.

It is time to recognize this unity that there is amongst you and us. It is time to be in allowance and doubt no further. Feel the presence of Divinity within you. Accept this truth to experience it.

There is an interconnectedness of all in existence.

Be gentle with yourselves. Have compassion for yourselves. Come forth in your newfound understanding to bring forth the light in you.

Set aside your logic. You are much deeper and much greater. You are the purity of the pure essence of God.

JOANNA ALEXOPOULOS

Recognize life as everlasting. Your authentic self, your soul, never dies. There is no death. There is life and there is life beyond, in an altered state, in an everlasting life of love with no suffering, with no limitations of the mind. The peaceful existence of your true self is that which you will return to.

It is time to understand that you can get to this place while still in your bodies, having your physical experiences. There is no need to pass on to return to who you really are. This is where your species is heading. Some have already reached it. This is the beautiful reality.

You are undergoing enormous shifts in consciousness that will take you to higher levels of thinking, new more advanced levels of understandings of life and who you are within it. Higher thought forms, inspiration for new developments, and ways of assisting each other to move out of the limitations of your minds are being presented to you. This is a wonderful time in your existence. Choose to bring it to you more quickly.

Be in allowance for higher-frequency energies to work through you. Accept this assistance and surrender to the unlimited possibilities that will filter through you, which will help you and your species to see things in the brightest light. Allow Divinity to work through you. Access and activate what is being offered you. There is hope. Grasp it now.

Spend time in nature. Spend more time being with the beauty that supports you. Connect to Mother Earth and the love that she is offering you. Be in the glory of life. Take the time to be in this stillness. The aliveness within you will be felt as the aliveness of your soul and will be awakened.

Spend time in nature. Remove your footwear. Remove what is blocking you from being in alignment with your higher self. Do

80

not block the flow. Allow the energy that is supporting you to heal you. Walk barefoot on your grasses to experience the deep connection of who you are. Feel and experience the beauty that surrounds you, for feeling is the language of who you really are. Ground yourself with that which you are made of. Heal yourselves. The time is now.

Create an oasis in your yards and your parks. Bask in the oneness of life. Get back into nature and take what is rightfully yours. Be one with life. Your planet is providing you with support. It is here for you to absorb. You have forgotten how.

Understand the connection you have, to all. You are oneness.

Thank Mother Earth for the love and support that she is giving each you, each and every day. Recognize this very important truth of your existence. Love her as she loves you. The time is now to assist in her healing.

Focus on what brings you joy, and lovingly give yourselves the time that you need to experience this. Stop all your busyness, with all your distractions, and draw yourselves back to what is most important.

Breathe in the universal oneness—the Divine connection that draws you all together. Take the time daily to go within. Focus on what really matters, and what really matters is you. It all starts with you.

As you go about your day, stop to visit your inner state. Stop and breathe. Breathe in the light and love of who you are.

You are compassion. You are love. You are magnificent beings of the totality of all in existence. You have the power to make what you want of your lives. You have the power to change your world, and you also have the power to destroy it.

You have the power to diminish, to damage, to inflict pain and suffering. You are living in a world full of hatred, with injustices of all kinds. Your species has proven your vile disregard with your horrific acts of violence and manipulation of your very own kind. This is not who you are. This is an extreme contradiction to your true nature. You are living through your insecurities.

The power is within you to either heal your world or continue as you have been.

The time is now to realize you are infinite beings with great potential. You are powerful manifesters.

Use your power to create abundance for all. Use your power to create a loving, compassionate world. Co-exist in a loving way, with compassion in your hearts and with the purity of innocence, for this is who you are. You are the innocence, the beauty, the light of God.

The time is now to take back your power. Move forward and upward. Realize the grand potentiality of who you are.

The time is now to rise and begin your personal inner transformation that will alter your thinking patterns and belief systems and change the minds of your world leaders.

The time is now to assist in the global awakening of your planet.

The time is now to take a stand. Your planet needs you.

Raise your vibrations. Be mindful to live your lives with awareness. Choose to be the best you can be each day. Make conscious choices to keep your vibration high.

Listen to music that uplifts you.

Watch programs on your televisions that are free from violent acts and injustices, free from anger and judgment, free from vengeful acts of betrayal, free from competition, free from greed.

Refrain from watching your news—anything that is not serving you, anything that is fostering an ill feeling within you. Be more mindful of what it is that frustrates you, angers you, and creates fear in you, for this is what is keeping you powerless. This is what is keeping your vibrational state low.

Take a step back and withdraw from engaging in all that does not build you up to be your best self. Release yourselves from the bondages of guilt, shame, and regret.

Raise your awareness and choose wisely. Where you will be is all in your choosing, and whichever state you choose is what you will attract and create more of. Choose wisely.

Take a stand and choose awareness. Take a stand and confirm to yourselves what it is you need to do to change yourselves to transform your world. Begin at this point by understanding there is great need.

Follow your hearts. Your heart will guide you, not your mind. Stop trying to logically think things through. Stop trying to figure it all out. There is no need. You will come to an understanding when you live with awareness. You will see more clearly. You will simply be, and your beingness will move mountains. The purest state of who you are will create the shift that will enable you to move into the direction that is most pleasing.

There need not be hunger. Many of your people are starving. There is no need. Assist your species in rising out of their impoverished states. The power is within you to assist your masses by simply raising your own awareness, by raising your own consciousness, by raising your personal vibrational frequency.

World hunger need not be. There is abundance for all. The universe supplies you with all that you need.

Manifest new desirable outcomes by being in a state of deliverance. Open your hearts to new possibilities. You are not stuck wherever you are. Be in a state of allowance, by freeing yourselves. Release the fear-based issues that are holding you from experiencing the truth of who you are.

Your species has not been mindful in assisting the growth of your planet. You have abused it as you have abused yourselves. The time is now to take charge of your lives. Rewind to recharge.

Your species has mistreated your home. You have carelessly allowed others to control it. You have left it in the hands of the very few, who have successfully managed to brainwash your masses. They are feeding you falsehoods, withholding the truth from you.

Suffering at the global level continues. Catastrophes plague your planet. There is dysfunction at all levels. Environmental devastation, starvation, terrorism, overpopulation, greed, and corruption feed the energy of your planet.

Wake up people. The time is now to take a stand.

Do not follow these corporate powers, for they are only interested in themselves. Do not continue to feed into these programs. Do not place your trust in the hands of organizations that have made little or no improvement for the collective. Support only what you know to be true. Be more knowledgeable to make a difference. Stop and think before you give openly. Know what you are supporting.

Corruption at the corporate level needs to stop. You are in the driver's seat to stop it. Do not support what they offer. Refrain from purchasing GMO products—produce that is ridden with chemicals and stripped of natural nutrients. Much of your soil is contaminated. This is killing you. World hunger continues. Nothing has improved.

On the evolutionary scale of development, you are going backwards. Stop destroying yourselves and your planet. Be prepared for much imbalance, as this is what you have created.

Rest assured you are supported by the heavens. You are always supported and even more so now. The awakening of your species is underway.

The time is now.

You are at the beginning of another millennium, which acts as a gateway of growth and opportunity. The universe is offering you transmissions of higher-frequency energies planting seeds of thought forms, inspiration, and mindfulness that will bring you to new heights. More and more of you are noticing.

Innovative practices will encourage profound transformation of all former practices. The delivery of these practices will be monitored by creative thinkers and implemented by those most open—those who have clarity in the overall transformation of global practices. More and more will be called upon to come forth. Inspiration will foster growth. There is much hope, as there is great need. It is your duty to implement your own practices to support this global awakening and transformation. Do your part in supporting what you know and understand to be true.

You are moving towards a more pleasing reality, one with hope, compassion, and peaceful resolution. The shift is happening, and we are so very pleased. You are moving out of the confusion, insecurity, and uncertainty of your darkest creations—of your world as you know it now. You are moving into a more blissful state.

Love is the highest vibration. Love will lead the way.

Be in allowance. Raise your consciousness to awaken to the truth of who you are. You are creative beings of loving kindness.

Move forward, one day at a time, and more and more will do their part in healing your world. Do not be concerned with those most resistant. They too will inevitably change their minds, as they will be more influenced by the energies around them. They too will be more interested in joining forces with those most vested in the goodness of humanity. Scientifically proven ground-breaking methodologies will satisfy those most unwilling. They will be supported by the influx of innovative practices that will move them out of their resistance.

This is what your future holds. There is great hope. There is promise for the healing of yourselves and your planet.

Focus more on you, and do not be so concerned with others. Your planet feels whatever vibration you are emanating. Be concerned with what you are putting forth—the higher your vibration, the greater your influence on all others.

More and more will come to a universal understanding of what it is that you need to do to bring yourselves out of this chaos of a world in which you are now living. This is not what you want. This is not who you are. The peace and harmony that you are seeking is within reach. We are here to remind you.

The time is now.

Be gentle and be mindful. You have all that you need within you. Access it now. Loving kindness is who you are.

Release your fears. Release all attachment to past situations. Release yourselves from those who have hurt you. Free yourselves from the bondage of your suffering states.

Fear no more, for this is what is holding you back. This is what is polarizing your planet. Live in the truth of who you are. Live in the moment, for this is what is real.

The choice is yours to either be in a place of love and joy and happiness or to be in a place of fear and desperation and loneliness. Choose to live in the moment. Choose to be happy. Choose love over fear, for this is who you are. Nothing else matters but your own personal state. It all begins with you and what you are feeling.

Choose to feel good and rejoice in the beauty of who you are. Cut the chords of attachment of past drama, and you will soon notice great shifts happening from deep within you.

One day at a time, one moment at a time, you will begin to feel the immense peace that you are. Make the choice to be happy, to foster new beginnings for yourselves and your species. You are oneness. Begin this transformation. You are well supported.

Understand you are not your mind. It is your egoic states with your self-righteous attitudes that keep you separate from one another. Drop your egos. This is not who you are. You are driving yourselves crazy. Your ego is feeding from your fearful states.

This is not who you are. You are much greater. You are the love and light that shines from within. This is who you are. Remember this truth.

Shine brightly, sweet ones. We are here supporting you every step of the way. Shine brightly, for you have not been forgotten. Begin now.

Great assistance from the heavenly realms is being poured upon you, infiltrating your consciousness, planting seeds of inspiration. Your minds are opening to new ideas each day. More and more are coming together in this oneness to heal your planet.

As you are coming into new understandings, you are finding the need and the drive to move forward and upward. More and more are coming together. More and more are re-membering.

One step at a time, your species will find your way again. You will rise to the beauty of who you are in your remembrance. Love will lead the way, not hatred. Peace will permeate your existence. There is great hope.

Look beyond the hatred, the disharmony of your planet and all its suffering. You will find the peace that you are. Take the time to recognize this truth. Do not be in judgment. It is within you.

Practice mindful awareness.

Focus on each moment. Slow yourselves down long enough to feel. Give yourselves the opportunity to be in the oneness of who you are, the interconnectedness of your existence. Be more present, for this is your present. Remember this, as this is your gift from God. Begin to see the beauty of life and the connection you have with All That Is.

Begin each day with hope and promise. Look for the beauty that surrounds you. Start with the awareness that you are the beauty and the love of God. This is who you are. Begin with this understanding to bring this back into your reality.

Practice feeding your consciousness loving thoughts, and you will begin the shift that is yours.

Surpass the negativity of your minds, for this is not who you are. You are not your minds. Change your minds to change your realities, mindfully choosing your thoughts one at a time. Be patient and be gentle. This is a process of your development.

Feed your minds with what really matters. No thing or person matters as much as you. Feed your minds with positivity, with happy thoughts, loving words, and with gratitude.

Vibrate high to attract high. Support your transformation to live the life that you deserve. Allow for all to unfold gently. Go with the flow of life. Do not resist what comes.

Be in alignment with the universal energies that support you. Allow magic to come to you.

As difficult a concept as this may appear, from whatever hardship, extreme situation, disease, or whatever it is that you are facing at this time, remember that it all begins with you and only you. It is your responsibility to bring yourselves back into alignment. No one else can do this for you.

Take one step at a time. Be with those who are on the same path. Be with those who can deliver the guidance and support that you need at this time. Bring yourselves out of the judgment, anger, or despair of whatever it is that you are experiencing. Be in allowance for inspiration to flow. Awareness fosters growth. Allow it to flow. Access it now.

Look for ways to help yourselves. There are many. Whatever resonates with you is the answer. Do not give up, for there is hope.

You are the greatest creators of all—an extension of God. You have been given the freedom to choose your way through life. Remember this, for this is the truth. You can alter your realities, if you so wish to, by choosing to alter your perception. Create a shift within you to experience differently.

You can heal every situation, every hardship, every form of disharmony of the body and of the mind. The power is within you. Remember this, for this is the truth.

Implement what you already have. Access what you have that lies within. Your time is now. Awaken to the beauty of who you are. We cannot stress this enough. We urge you to deliver to yourselves what is rightfully yours.

This suffering at your personal and global levels has gone on far too long. The time is now to allow your consciousness to soar to new heights, to facilitate the transformation of your planet.

Offer the love that you have to yourselves. Draw from it the highest vibration that is yours in connection to the Divinity that you are. You are all worthy. You are the light. You are the essence of purity and innocence.

Come together and reunite. Come together in celebration of your becoming. It is yours to experience. Awaken to this beautiful truth. You are wonderful beings of light.

Practice what you know. Follow your hearts. Intuitively, you know where to begin. Begin at this place. Feel and trust, for you will not be steered wrongly. Follow your hearts, as this is who you are. Follow what feels good from your heart-centered consciousness, and trust that this is where you need to be.

Go within and feel what is right for you. Release the fear that is holding you back, for this is not love. This is not who you are. Release this to feel what is right for you, for only you know. Trust in the guidance system that exists within you.

If this is foreign to you, begin by acknowledging your truth. Recognize the light in you to begin your process, for this is a process—a process of growth and expansion of your consciousness.

Place your focus and energy on what will bring you closer to the God essence in you. Place your intention where it needs to be, and this will drive your energy. Focus on what matters, and what matters is you. You are what matters. Focus on yourselves to help each other, for you are all connected.

Maintain your balance. Support the inner truth that you are by being open for new beginnings to flow. Create within yourselves the space for growth that is longing to unfold, for this is a process—an evolutionary process of your development.

Recognize the immobilization of humanity. Recognize that many are not in allowance, living in their egoic states, unable to see past themselves. Take responsibility and recognize that you have the power to make a difference. Assist those who are still living in their dormant stages. Maintain your balance and allow your light to shine on others. The power is within you.

The choice is yours. Allow yourselves the opportunity for growth that is awaiting you. Accelerate your ascension. Do not be in resistance, as this will stagnate your growth. Allow the love from within you to surface. The time is now to grasp this opportunity that lies before you. The time is now for the expansion of your consciousness.

Awaken to empower yourselves to make more elevated choices, with clarity of life and its universal truths. Know who you are to realize your potentiality, for you are the most powerful creators. Recognize this truth within you.

Practice moment-to-moment awareness to remove that which is obstructing you from moving forward, for it is your negative thought forms that are limiting you, keeping you in a paralyzed state. Open your minds to open yourselves up to your greatest potentiality.

You are limitless. You are expansive. You are not within the boundaries of your limitations, for there are none.

Be the creators that you are meant to be. Free yourselves from the cultural, religious, social, and family biases that are holding onto you. This is not who you are. You are much greater. Release yourselves from the victimhood mentalities that you have placed on yourselves. Release yourselves from the blame and the shame, from the guilt and the doubt, from all your insecurities that are holding you back. Release yourselves, for you and only you have the power to do so.

Live in the moment. Recognize the resiliency, the flexibility, and the impermanency of every single moment. This is what is real.

Understand you are in control of your moments. It is you who can alter them and create new ones. Do not hold yourselves hostage to past moments, as they are not real. They no longer exist. Create new moments to create new beginnings, for only then can you realize and access the potentiality of who you are.

The sooner you believe, the sooner you may set yourselves free. Believe this to access your power. Choose to lift yourselves out of the discomfort of your past hurts and judgments.

Stop living in the past. Remove yourselves from your suffering states by simply changing your minds. Cut the cords of attachment to any and all your past. Cut the chords of attachment to anything that is not serving you. Change your minds to change your realities. Alter your thinking one moment at a time. Ask for guidance. It is there.

Express gratitude for where you are now. This will assist your process of self-discovery, with the emergence of a much-higher frequency that will give you that release and peace you are looking for.

You are not victims. You are not stuck in the past, unless you choose to be. You are making yourselves believe there is no other way. This is the biggest misconception, for there are many other ways.

Anchor each moment with gratitude to accelerate your healing process. Affirm to yourselves the beauty of what surrounds you.

Find the truth of who you are by anchoring the light within you. Focus on all that you are thankful for each day. For many of you it is easier to journal. Begin your gratitude journal to foster and create shifts in your consciousness.

The time is now to begin your own personal process. The time is now to change your minds to change not only your reality but others, as you are co-creators in this world of duality. Change your minds to change your world. The time is now. Your species is in a suffering state that has created a world of dysfunction, self-absorption, and self-indulgence.

Live in your truth to free yourselves of your suffering states.

Change your minds to heal yourselves and your planet. Understand you are not victims. Create with the understanding that you are who you choose to be.

Do not return to something you no longer are. Create from a place of openness and understanding of your greatest truth—you are the children of God, the greatest creators of all. Realize this truth to realize your potentiality.

Be in a place of allowance. Allow your Divine energy to flow. Open yourselves to your creativity. Create ... for this is the reason you came here.

Be in a place of awareness to create the movement toward transformation—transformation for your entire planet. The time is now.

Forgive all who have harmed you. Forgiveness will transcend the hurt within you. Consciously find it in your hearts to be in this space of forgiveness—forgiving yourselves and others for the hurt, the pain, and the suffering you have allowed to enter your lives.

93

All the heartache, the blame, the anger, the resentment of what someone did to you, what someone said to you, and what happened to you is creating more and more pain and suffering. This is not allowing you to move forward. Do not resist. Your pains are stepping stones to greater experiences.

Those who have hurt you are not in this remembrance. It is you. Release what is blocking you from experiencing the joy of life. Release the anger and the resentment to free yourselves. This is not who you are. You are much greater.

Do not hang on to what is not supporting you. Do not live in the truth of negativity. Do not live in the limitations created by the illusions of who you are not. Release this mindset to set yourselves free.

Do not define yourselves by what has happened to you. This will keep you in a place of non-deliverance. Fully accept to transcend. Embrace it, learn from it, and let it go.

Forgiveness will set you free.

Bring yourselves out of the darkness to see the light. You are the light—the light of all existence. Change your minds to change your behaviors, which will change your realities. Alter your thinking to create new beginnings. Those closest to you remain in the darkness with you, watching you in this misery, picking up the energy of your darkness, of your pain ... of your suffering.

Free yourselves. Free each other. Choose differently.

Forgive yourselves, for without your personal forgiveness, there is no love for yourselves and no love for others. Love is the ultimate force. Love has the power to transform. Forgive yourselves to regain your power.

Blame no one. Open to new possibilities. Blame will keep you locked in self-pity. This is not who you are. Move out of the darkness of your creations to experience the love and light of who you are. Set yourselves free.

Be the Light
Be the Love
Be the Glory
For in this Truth
Lie the Answers
To All

7
The Universe Is Listening

Divine support is available to you. Divinity is assisting you every step of the way. We are supporting you in moving out of your confusion, your insecurities, and your fears and into a more loving, healing, and trusting awareness. We are here to assist you in your awakening to the highest truth of who you are. The time is now to seize your power, one step at a time.

Begin now from wherever you are. Begin to make the changes within you to create the transformation for humanity that will change everything. Prepare for mass awakening. Soon you will know yourselves differently from a more expanded perspective. You will experience differently. You will live your lives, interact with each other, treat your environment, conduct your businesses, educate your children, build relations and govern your world differently.

Accelerate your process. Catch yourselves from the compulsive-thinking minds of your egos. Catch yourselves in the negative-thinking patterns that are holding you back. Catch yourselves, and with the glory of your becoming, alter your thinking to create the shift that will transform the habitual, limiting patterning of your minds. Catch yourselves and change your minds. The power is in within you.

Think and speak more mindfully. Slow yourselves down long enough to make conscious decisions that will determine how you live your lives. Mindful awareness will bring you to the peace you are looking for. Speak with the intention of producing the results that will enhance you—that will bring results that will uplift you and those around you. Be more mindful to create the experiences that will support your growth.

Do your part in the creation process, and you will notice the changes in you bring about changes in others. Speak kindly. Speak gently. Have compassion, for you are all on different paths in your evolutionary processes. Be loving and be kind to each other to help each other develop and grow into the beauty of who you really are.

Be patient, as this is a process—a process of your development.

Give yourselves the space and time that you need to heal from past hurts. Give yourselves what you need. Lovingly accept yourselves wholly and completely as the purity of who you are. Begin your process of self-discovery and self-development. Begin now, for this is your time to save yourselves and your planet. It all starts with you.

Make the conscious choice to bring about change—the change you wish to see for yourselves, for others, and for your planet. This is all in your power.

Acceptance will set you free.

Understand you have no power over what others do and how they live their lives. This is not in your control. Manage your own lives by managing your thinking minds. Do not be so concerned with the doings of others, as they are manifesters of their own paths, living in the realities of their own choosing.

Focus on your own lives, and with love in your hearts, one step at a time, you will directly influence the lives of others. Be an example for others to follow. Shine your light in the darkness, and one step at a time, more and more will be influenced by you, as you are all interconnected.

Create within yourselves that which you know you are. Go within and anchor the light of your existence, for you are the light—the light of God.

The anger, the judgment, and the blame that permeates and plagues your planet is not who you are. Do not identify with the energy of that which you are not. The time is now to fully embrace your true essence—love. Remember this truth to begin to withdraw yourselves from what does not enhance you, what does not raise you up. Realize this and change your minds to change your realities.

Fully accept where you are at this moment. Do not condemn yourselves. Love yourselves with all that you are and fully open your hearts. With the power of love, the beauty of love will begin the shift to assist you in your awakening.

The power is within you. Convince yourselves that you are more than you know. You are more than the physicality of your existence. You are much greater. You are expansive, creative energy. You have the ultimate power within you ... to be, do, and have whatever you wish, for you are a part of the unified field of existence. You are a part of God.

Embrace this truth to change your world. Move to a more glorified field of existence. You have the power to do so, and it all starts with each one of you.

Take part in this grand movement towards unification of all. Accept where you are and begin your own movement that will not only help yourselves but help all. Surrender to the beauty of who you are. Embrace it.

The hurt, the pain, and the suffering need not be your identity. Release that which you are not. Release what is not serving you. Let go of what is blocking you. Change your minds. Change your attitudes to change your behaviours. This will alter your realities, for it is your limiting beliefs about yourselves and your world that have brought your home to this place of darkness.

Challenge yourselves. Open your hearts. Grasp the vibration that is the essence of your truth. Convince yourselves.

There is hope and there is promise for new wonderful beginnings. You are the light and love of God. Trust and you will experience the joy of who you are and the glory of your existence. Your truth is inside you.

Do not focus on what is not working for you as this will keep you in a state of non-deliverance. Do not be so in your minds. You are using your minds mindlessly. You are exerting too much energy on what you are not wanting.

Accept yourselves and all that you are facing. This will place you in the receiving mode—one which will open the door for Divinity of who you are to flow through you. This will embrace your creative energy that will give you the clarity that you need to harness the intuitive intelligence of who you are. Your answers are there, inside you. Be more in allowance.

Accept yourselves as you are. Accept all around you as it is. Accept your situations, as difficult as they are. Fully accept your reality in order to transform and transcend it. This is the only way.

Acceptance is the only way.

Allow all the hurt, all the anger, and all the judgment to pass through you. Release it, as this is not yours. This is an illusion of the identity of who you are not.

You are not your mind. You are much greater. Trust that you are more than this. You are greater than all the negativity that is around you. Your intuitive intelligence will guide you from wherever you are. Trust in yourselves, for you have the power to create new beginnings, to change who you are and how you view your world.

Get out of your minds to get into your hearts. From this place, you will have an inner sense of knowingness of what you need to do to move forward. Your heartfelt centre is your core of creation. From here, be open, be ready, and be in allowance of receiving the energy that will transform you. For this is the energy, the highest of frequencies, of your Godly nature.

The core of who you are is deep within you. Anchor this energy to bring it to the light, for humanity has been forever in the darkness of your destructive creations.

Your suffering states have not gone unnoticed. Make the choice to help yourselves. The time is now.

Surrender to what is rightfully yours. Free yourselves from the prisons of your minds. You have committed yourselves to the pain that has become your realities. All the disease and disharmony of the body and of the mind have come from an illusion of who you are not. You are not this dysfunction. Do not own whatever ailment. Do not allow it to become a part of you.

Understand fully that you can shift into new directions. You can remove yourselves from any and all imbalance. You can uplift and transform yourselves. You have the ultimate power to heal yourselves. Begin now. Love yourselves, as it all begins with love.

Love is the answer.

Love is your highest truth. Love who you are. See yourselves as the love of who you are. Convince yourselves, as this is your truth. You are all this essence—all of you.

You are all the children of God. You all have the God-spark energy within you. You are all this light.

You are all loved and accepted unconditionally. You are God's children, and He loves you all, with all your shortcomings, with your perceived faults, with your suffering states, with your lacks and your wants, with all your broken parts.

God loves you all, and God always sees you all for who you are: a part of Him, Divinity expressing itself fully.

The choice is yours, for this is a choice. Become the best you can be. Experience the most expansive model of yourself. It is for you to access. Make the choice to make the shift—the shift in consciousness that will enable you to access the power that waits to unfold from deep within you.

The choice is yours, and the time is now.

Love yourselves as you are. Affirm to yourselves that you are the love that you are. Remind yourselves, for you have forgotten.

Affirm to yourselves throughout your day, "I am light. I am love. I am that I am," as this will transform you.

Change your beliefs about yourselves to change your realities. Convince yourselves to change your stories. Affirm to yourselves to change your minds, for you have forgotten.

Begin the inner transformation that awaits you. It is in your choosing to experience the Divine nature in you.

Do not be so confused. It all starts with you.

Accept where you at this moment. Accept it, for you have created it.

It is you who has brought to you whatever it is you are experiencing at this time. It is you, with your thought forms, your belief systems, through your past programming, and your soul decision for your personal expansion. Believe this, as this is the truth.

Surrender to what is before you. Fully accept where you are to transcend it. Understand you have total control.

Forgive yourselves. You are not meant to suffer. Your journey entails experience and growth. Be in this remembrance.

Do not go about your lives forcefully plugging through to your next moments. Do not go through your lives without much awareness. Life is not meant to be a struggle.

With forceful creation comes disappointment, frustration, anxiety, anger, bitterness, and disease. Forceful creation is not serving you. It is inhibiting you from bountiful creation, that which you so deserve.

All of what you want for yourselves is within reach. There is no need to force your way into what you wish. The power is within you. Feel your way into your tomorrows. Place yourselves in vibrational harmony with that which you want. This is the way to receive it.

Empower yourselves with your vibrations. There is nothing you need to do. You just need to *be* ... be more present.

Believe in yourselves. Follow your inner guidance. Do what you love. Follow your dreams and you will not be disappointed. Do not force your way through your lives. Guide them with passion and with love in your hearts.

You did not come into physicality to forcefully lead and control your lives. You came to create from a loving peaceful state, with your intentions and your feelings. This is the energy of powerful creation.

Humanity has not been living through the infinite potentiality of who you are. You have been struggling, living in the limited thinking patterns of your minds.

Do not be in denial.

It is time to awaken and recognize that you, as a collective, are responsible for where you are globally. You are responsible for the heart-breaking condition of your planet.

Your lives are not the most pleasant. Your planet is not functioning the most efficiently. You are responsible for your disharmony, as it is as a direct result of your mindless creations. You are creating unconsciously.

Come to an understanding that it is you who can change this.

Life is vibration. Thought is vibration. Choose to emanate in the highest vibration. Focus on the light, not on the darkness. Choose the vibration that will bring you the most pleasing experiences that will bring your planet the most pleasing results.

Bring yourselves to where you are truly yearning to be.

You all want to attain things that will provide you with more comfort. Raise your vibrations to be more in allowance. This is the way.

Allow life to work for you, not against you.

Be more aware of the vibration you are choosing. You will be swallowed into the vortex of this vibration. Choose wisely.

Believe more in what you want to attract it. It is within reach. See yourselves within it. Feel it. Feel the vibration of it. Allow it to come to you. The more you believe, without resistance, without doubt and insecurity, the easier and faster you will attract it.

With love in your hearts, with gratitude, with confidence and trust, you may bring to you whatever it is that you desire. It is that simple. This is the truth.

You are all in vibration, creating and shaping your experiences together.

You are creating from a place of fear. You are creating without love for each other and without love for your planet.

You are killing each other with your thoughts, words and deeds. You are killing your home. You are living in a low state as a result of the negativity formed from the beliefs that you live by. Understand this fully.

The time is now to make a change that will influence the vibration of your planet in a more positive, loving direction.

There is no need to plead. There is no need to justify bringing what you want into your experience. God is listening. There is no need to shed tears. The Universe is listening. Your angels and guides are listening. God's Divine family is listening.

Place your focus and intention on that which you wish to bring to you. Do not remain locked, stuck in the vibration of lack and unworthiness. Focus your attention with gratitude, faith, trust, and openness and you will receive it all.

This is how life works. Make a choice on how you want your life to be. The universe is listening and responding to whatever you are putting forth.

You are all deserving. You are of light and love, worthy and deserving of everything that you wish for. Remember this. The choice is yours to either live in fear or live in love.

Create from a place of faith ... and trust. Strengthen your faith. Surrender to the unknown. Meditate to find your peace. It is there.

Trust in the unknowingness. God is within reach. He is a part of you.

You are a part of God's family, and He loves you dearly.

Train your mind to think more loving thoughts. Change your mind to allow goodness to enter. Feed your mind what it needs, to be in allowance for your creative energy to flow and create the world that is most pleasing to you.

The time is now for healing and exploration. Where are you now? Where are you heading as an individual and more importantly as a collective?

It is not too late. All the dysfunction that plagues you, all the chaos your species is experiencing, can be reversed when you are willing to make this transition. You can reverse the direction of your future, and you can do it now, as fast as you want it. It is your responsibility, no one else's. We encourage you to bring yourselves back into alignment.

The time is now.

Return yourselves to the peace that you know you are. There is no need for conflict. There is no need for competition. This is not grade school. There is no need for judgment. See yourselves as the love that you are, as the glory of God's creation, each one of you. Help yourselves to remember who you are. Your species has lost its way.

Accept each other's differences and unite with compassion. You will be rewarded greatly.

Remember this truth to set yourselves free—free from the inner turmoil of your egoic states. You are not your mind. You are much greater.

You are Source energy beings living in physicality to create and experience life fully, to grow and expand and become brighter and brighter. The sooner you understand this, the sooner you can rejoice and return to your natural states. You are the beauty, the love, the morality, the kindness. You are supreme beings. Your species need not continue in this suffering state.

Wake up to this truth in acceptance of what God has given you, for this is the light and the truth of who you are. Love is your natural state, no other.

Return yourselves to your natural state to return to yourselves the world that you deserve—a world that is abundant without injustice, disharmony, separation, lack, pain, and sorrow that plagues your planet today.

Your time is now to heal your world. Return it to its natural state.

We are here to assist you in your awakening, bringing forth wisdom that will ignite your conscious minds into questioning and longing for more insight. Spark energy will ignite each one of you, one at a time, when the time is right for each and every one of you—when you are ready.

Be in remembrance
Begin in the truth of who you are
Infinite flow awaits you
Transferring unlimited Source energy

Fruition of all creations
Multiply in the glory of pure intention
The connection is yours

8
Journey Through Life

Be in remembrance you are not your thoughts. Your thoughts are energy patterns of habitual mindsets. Your thoughts are stored belief systems that are not real. They are telling you stories that do not serve you.

They are telling you that you are not enough. You are not good enough, you are not smart enough, you are not successful enough, you are not thin enough ... that you are less than.

This is your ego mind telling you to stay where you are. This is what is comfortable. This is what is safe. This is what it knows. It is the *you* protecting *you*, for this is what you know and understand from a lifetime of habit from others' thoughts, opinions, and beliefs, having stored them in your cellular memories from your families, your cultures, your religions, your educators, your relationships, your communities ... from all those around you that have contributed in molding and shaping you. This is what resides within you.

Understand that you have been living under the influences of others. All that is stored in your memory banks have created the mindsets that you have now. You have acquired them as your own as you have not allowed yourselves the freedom to open your minds and explore.

The time is now to start thinking for yourselves. The time is now to open your minds to view life differently. The time is now to redirect your pessimistic inner dialogue. The time is now to clear it.

With conscious effort and intention, you can stop this replay of chatter. Stop what is distracting and overpowering you. Realize now that you are not what your mind is telling you. Grasp the power that you truly are.

The choice is yours to begin to transform this inner dialogue. The time is now to understand who you truly are and turn that energy around.

All that is stored in your memory is blocking the freedom that you are. The time is now to shed these attachments and open your minds to greater understandings.

Your mind will continue to categorize, criticize, and replay all the scenarios of your past and your conditioned beliefs about them. Your mind has great power over you when you allow it. Know you are beyond your mind and know that you can transform it.

The choice is yours when you are ready to embark on something new. You can change your story. The choice is yours when you have had enough ... when you are ready to break away from the prison of your mind.

Take more care with what you are thinking. Be more responsible with the energy you are transmitting. Thought has the greatest power to manifest things and events in your lives. Thought has the power to mold your experiences. Think what you are producing and create what you are really wanting.

With intention, practice and patience, you can shift the delusions and illusions of your past that have shaped you. This is not who you are. Place your focus on where you really want it to be. You are not what your mind is telling you.

Do not wait for others. Do not wait for others to fix things for you. Do not put yourselves in a waiting game, for this is a false perception. Help yourselves by taking full responsibility for the state of mind that you are in. Raise your awareness. You are in full control. Create your best life.

The victim perspective is a false understanding. You are not victims. Your species tends to believe you are. This is suppressing your natural state.

Do not live with regret, frustration, and anger. Do not focus on what has happened to you. Grow from wherever you've been and know you will get to wherever you need to be with faith and with trust.

Trust in the greatness of who you are and who you are becoming. Know that you are greater than the limitations you have placed upon yourselves.

Blame no one—not yourselves, nor anyone that you feel has contributed to your low states at this time. Blame is a fear-based perspective that will keep you locked in your misery. Be more present in your moments and create with the love that you are. You are Source energy beings. Remember this truth.

The present moment is what is real. The present moment is the point place of all creation, for it is from the present moment that you can create and shift your realities into different directions.

Trust that you are not alone. You are loved and you are supported by a greater power. Begin to create and experience the love that you are, from a loving, forgiving place, without the darkness and pain of your suffering. Move forward now.

Believe you are blessed. Believe you are powerful. Believe you are successful. Believe this to experience it. Affirm it to yourselves. "I am blessed. I am powerful. I am successful." Repeat it over and over again to make yourselves believe the truth of who you really are. Convince yourselves. You have forgotten.

You are nothing less than the beauty of all in existence.

The time is now to regain your focus and place your attention and intention on creating movement for change. It all starts with you.

Gratitude will take you there. Begin your day with focused attention.

"Thank you, God, for my life. Thank you, God, for my family. Thank you, God, for my home. Thank you for all that I have and more."

Look around you. You will see your abundance. Look around and notice the amenities in your life: the running water, the roof over your heads, the comforts that you have that have enabled you to live more fully with ease and comfort. Continue throughout your day feeling your way with gratitude in your hearts.

Gratitude will take you to new heights of awareness. This will raise your vibration.

Remember that it is up to you, each one of you. It is your choice in moving yourselves to greater heights to experience the greatness of who you are and move yourselves into more freedom.

We encourage you to change your minds. You are not the pain and the suffering that you have made yourselves believe. You are the joy and the love. Accept yourselves. You are enough. You are more than enough. You are greatness.

Allow yourselves to see more clearly. Bring yourselves out of your self-doubt, out of your limitations. All will fall into place as you continue to realign yourselves with your true nature. Abundance will continue to flow and unfold. One by one, your inner-guidance support systems will be activated from their dormancy states.

Trust that we are here to guide and support you. We are here with you every step of the way.

You are in physical form to experience. You are on a journey of ascension. You have incarnated to evolve.

Understand you have come to feel and experience life as you attract it. Whatever comes to you comes for broader understandings. You have come with your own personal agendas to learn what you need to learn, for the expansion of your true selves—your souls.

You are on an expansive journey of growth and development. See yourselves in this way. Do not contract the energy that you are made of.

Attain the wisdom that you are. Your life is a process of development on your healing journey.

You are all at different stages in your growth, in your understandings of life, in your consciousness; however, you all want the same. You want to live an abundant life with equity, peace, and harmony.

The time is now to awaken to the unlimited potentiality of who you are. We cannot stress this enough. There is no need to live within the boundaries you have set for yourselves. There is no need to live in a robotic state, without joy in your lives. Return yourselves to your true essence to live more fully.

Stop the worry, the doubt, and the fear that permeates and rules your existence. Live in the now moment. This is where change begins. Set your thoughts in motion with emotion of what you are asking, with love. Set this in motion to access opportunities that will enhance your lives and others. You are all connected. Create a new world for yourselves.

You are worthy and deserving, and yes, you are all enough ... you just haven't understood it.

Do not minimize your importance. Do not keep finding faults with yourselves. Stop the constant judgment as this is not benefiting your advancement. Understand the truth of who you are. Understand the perfection that you are for when you judge yourselves you are closing yourselves off from the unlimited potentiality of who you can become. You are constantly growing and expanding. This is your purpose. Allow yourselves to achieve what you came here for.

Do not be so hard on yourselves. Your mind is taking you to places which are not in your truth. Realize your self-worth to access and activate your personal power. Create the shift that will alter your mindsets about yourselves. Allow yourselves the freedom to become your greatest selves in this lifetime.

Darkness permeates your planet—the dark energy of fear. Fear has been the source of your creations. Bring your planet out of this darkness. Return yourselves to the love that you essentially are.

The time is now.

The need for power and control has consumed your species. There is an inherent need to control, to safeguard what you believe to be rightfully yours. There is an innate fear of loss, and this is all in line with the belief that you are separate in and of each other. When you believe in this separation, you inherently feel the need to protect.

This is a very limited mindset, a primitive belief that is causing humanity much anxiety. You believe you need to protect, whether it is yourselves, your families, your religions, your cultures, or your nations. There is a very strong need to protect what is rightfully yours, as you believe it to be within the boundaries of yourselves. This has altered your natural state. This has suppressed your independence. This inherent need for protection and control has ruptured the fabric of your existence.

You are not separate. You are oneness, made of the same particles—of God. You are one with All That Is, with everyone and everything on your planet, above it and below it, with everything including your universe and galaxies.

We are all connected. Believe this, as this is the absolute truth.

Do not criticize. Do not blame others, expecting them to make changes. Realize it is you who needs to take more responsibility. It is you who needs to be more aware of what you can do to facilitate in the healing of your personal world and that of your planet.

Understand that there will be no positive improvements—no shifts until you raise your vibrations. Operating at a much higher frequency is your answer. This will bring you out of your suppressed states of disempowerment.

You have given up your power and have allowed others to lead you.

Those in control of your nations, those who manage your governments, those who have the power over you to control your lives and make decisions for you, those to whom you have given up your power are those who are contributing greatly to your downfall. Understand that your world leaders have very different agendas from the collective. Their interests are different from yours.

In this co-creative world, resistance penetrates and fosters your realities. You cannot create effectively when you are not on the same wave-length—when you are not in the same vibration.

Elevate yourselves to be in the vibration that will create positive change for the collective.

Control is not your answer.

Just as your world leaders control your masses, many of you control your children, with the intention of protection.

There is no need to manage and control others. There is no need to protect, for you are all protected. There is no need to live in fear.

Manage only yourselves. Trust that you are not separate from each other. All that you think, say, and do contributes to the vibration of your planet. Every thought you have is creating an energy that not only affects your personal vibration but your global.

Many of you are in wanting but are not in a state of allowance. The energies created by you have not served you. Change your vibrations. You are creative beings living in physicality to experience yourselves fully. This is a beautiful reality. Embrace it now.

Stop living with uncertainty. This is creating chaos amongst you. Stop living in resistance. You are attracting what you least desire. You are living your lives with false hopes and promises.

The time is now to awaken to new possibilities.

Bring yourselves out of your fear-based states. This is not who you are. There is no need to give up your power and follow others. You are not separate. Do not follow those who believe they are.

Unite in oneness. Stand strong and help one another. Do not follow blindly. Do not trust when one speaks of separation, using comparisons and condemnation of others and other ways. Do not follow those who believe their way is the only way, for the only way is through your own individual way going within, following your heart. This is the only way to inner peace and transformation. Love is the only way. Find your God within. This is where He is.

Live your lives more peacefully. Understand that you are all different, and this is a beautiful reality. Understand that you are all unique and special, and you all have different gifts to share. Understand that you are all at different stages of your soul developments and understand that this is perfectly fine. Understand that you are one unit, and you are here together to live together in peace and in harmony.

Be mindful of the energy you put forth. Raise the vibration of your planet by doing your part to heal yourselves, to heal your world. Listen intently and follow only those who have love in their hearts. See the unity of all in existence. You are not separate.

Create and co-create from this understanding. It is within you to offer what you have, what you have been given from Source. See the unity of all in existence. You are not separate. You are one with God.

Your hospitals are full of what you have created. They are full of those you have not understood the meaning of life—those who have allowed themselves to be swallowed by the negativity of their minds.

It is time to understand deeper truths to reverse the damage that you have created.

Your species has made yourselves sick with self-doubt and worry. Your beliefs about yourselves have failed you. Inevitably, you fall off the wagon of life ... and then you give up. You give up on life and fall into victimhood. You tend to blame yourselves, and you put blame on others.

This need not be.

Listen to your bodies. Feel what your body needs. Listen to your hearts. Stay focused long enough to feel.

Understand that you cannot help yourselves when you give up your power.

Wake up people. You are making yourselves sick. Take responsibility.

Your hospitals are full of like-minded, lost people, people who have given up, people who have a limited view of who they are. This need not be.

Surrender, for this is the ultimate state of allowance. Surrender is your answer—surrender in order to allow the current of life to bring you out of your disharmony. Surrender from being in a state that is not to your liking. Understand this as not giving up. This is letting go. It is being in a state of allowance.

The choice is yours, and the choice is simple. Change your minds to change your lives. The time is now. Do not hold back. Do not hold onto the mistakes that you believe you have made. Refrain from reliving your past negative experiences. Live with hope, not regret.

Live for the now, for this is where you can shift into newer realities.

Return yourselves back to yourselves. Take yourselves out of your hospitals and awaken to the power that you are. Heal yourselves. Trust that you have what it takes. You have the ultimate power. Change your minds to change your lives.

The time is now to raise your vibrations. Play with the energies of life. Understand that you are in complete control of what you vibrate.

Your vibration emanates what you think, feel, believe, and speak. It is the frequency of your personal energy. Your cells vibrate at the frequency that you allow yourself to be in. The higher your frequency, the more insight and awareness you will have and the more light you will hold. You will be healthier, and your lives will run more smoothly as you will be in alignment with the Divine perfection of who you are—your intuitive intelligence.

The time is now to reclaim your energy and create new beginnings for yourselves and your planet. Heal your world. You are spiritual beings. You are much more than your physical bodies.

Be more aware of your energetic bodies and what you vibrate. Do not allow yourselves to vibrate at low states. Do not allow yourselves to be in the darkness and heaviness, operating from your lower selves—operating from your fears and insecurities.

Practice non-judgment.

Do not judge yourselves. You tend to be your biggest critics. Have no regrets. See yourselves as whole, as you are complete. You are complete in your creation, as you are an extension of God and He sees you as whole. Release yourselves of all the heartache that you have created in your minds. You are complete, and you are whole. There is nothing that you are not.

Do not judge yourselves. Do not judge others. Life is a process of development, and you are all going through your processes. Making mistakes along the way is all within the process of self-discovery. See yourselves in this way, as you are all learning and growing, some more quickly, others more slowly. You are all in this process of healing, evolving through your experiences.

The pain of your past need not define your future. Be more compassionate and take better care of yourselves. You have complete control of your future by thinking differently in your present. You are not your past. Set yourselves free.

Change your minds to change your realities, and this will change your world.

We see too many of you living in pain, swallowed with regret and self-pity, day after day ... waiting for something that is outside of you to change, something that may lift you out of your depressed states.

This is not how life works.

Raise your vibrations to be on the same wavelength as your soul, as this is where you will find your peace. This is where you will find opportunity. This is where abundance will flow. Find the love that you are. Go within. Be in the silence of who you really are. This is the secret of all creation.

Love yourselves enough to see the light in you. Accept yourselves as you are. Breathe in the freshness of your existence. Miracles will flow to you, one after another. You will experience the beauty of who you are with all that it has to offer.

Be in alignment with your soul. Raise your vibrations to experience yourselves fully.

Release all judgment of yourselves and others. Begin with a clean slate, with the understanding that you are complete, you are loved, and you are whole. There is nothing you are not. With this clarity, move forward.

Mindfully raise your vibrations. Remind yourselves of your unlimited potentiality. Fully embrace the joy of gratitude. Remind yourselves of your good fortunes, for there is much to be grateful for. Awaken to who you are.

Stop your distractions and mindfully embrace yourselves as the soul creators that you are. Gratitude will reset your minds. You will begin to see things differently.

Be in this remembrance, as you have forgotten. Reprogram your thinking patterns.

Your planet is suffering. It is not in balance, as your species is not. Raise your vibrations to elevate your consciousness, to assist in transforming the consciousness of your planet. Practice mindfulness. Keep your frequency high to assist in the planetary shift.

You are not alone on this venture.

Each one of you has a multitude of angels assisting you, helping you stay focused, to be the best you can be, lovingly guiding and supporting you without judgment. Know in your hearts that you are not alone. God is with you.

God loves you and has forgiven you for all your misgivings. God sees the light in you at all times.

Open your hearts and be in allowance for love to flow. This is who you are. Be in this remembrance to allow the love that you are to resonate and permeate within you and around you. Love is your power. This is what you will return to. This is what will transform your world.

The forgetfulness that fosters your species is keeping you in a state of disempowerment. Remember you are the power. You are the power of all creation. Each one of you has the power. Be in this remembrance, and with love in your hearts, create the world you wish to live in.

Make adjustments in allowance for spirit to work through you. Take time in your day to be in a peaceful state. Quiet your minds to hear your answers. You are connected. We are connected. Your realm and ours are connected. There is no separation.

Heal yourselves and your world with the innate power that you are. Free yourselves from the compulsive thinking patterns of your minds to liberate yourselves and experience your true essence.

Allow the light of who you are to come forth, to deliver you the grace and glory of life. Create from the knowingness that you are sovereign beings, for you are directly connected to universal energy, to God, to Source—to the power of all creation.

Find your power within. Reclaim it. It is yours. Do not look elsewhere. You are the power. Create from this place, and you will be rewarded greatly. Feel the love that you are, for this is where you will find your peace. This is how you will live fully. This is where all will fall into place and nothing will be in your experience but that which you are wanting. This is where you will come to new understandings about who you are.

Looking elsewhere, giving up your power to others, and living from a place of fear and uncertainty has not served you. It has created anger, guilt, blame, shame, doubt, unforgiveness, greed, addiction, and separation amongst you.

Be more mindful of your thinking patterns, more respectful of your words, more compassionate with your actions. This is where it all begins. Love who you are to create the shift that is awaiting you, which will change the energy of your entire planet. Raise your vibrations with love energy, the most powerful energy of all. This is the energy that you are looking for—the energy that many of you have forgotten.

Love who you are, with all your perceived faults.

You are not broken. You are whole. You are complete. You need healing. Be in this remembrance to bring yourselves back to yourselves.

Nothing is greater than inner peace. Nothing.

Set aside your worries. Set aside your insecurities. Do not believe you are less than.

God sees you as the pure essence of love, regardless of where you have been and what you have done. God sees you as light, today and every day.

Each minute of each day is a new beginning. It is a new creation. Life is fluidity. Allow expansive energy to flow.

Do not continue making yourselves sick with worry and doubt. Alter your thinking to create room for change. Come out of this place of darkness that is holding you back. You are all worthy.

Come out of this density. Your planet is suffering. Raise your vibrations to assist your planet in rebalancing itself. The shift is happening. Come together with this awareness to speed up this process, for this is a process—a process of your evolution.

You are abundant. You are worthy. Believe this and be open and receptive to allow it to enter your lives. God has given you free will. The choice is yours.

See each other with love in your hearts. Do not be in judgment of those who are not like you. Celebrate your differences, for this is the beauty of life's creations. You are made of the same spark, made of universal light, made of love energy, made of God.

Do not be in judgment.

Love your neighbor, for he is like you. He is managing the best he can within the limitations of his mind. Do not be in judgment. Love your neighbor as you love yourselves. You are all God's children. Remember this, for when you are in judgment, you are also judging yourselves.

Create more fully. Do not contract your energy. Embrace the love that you are. You are not the fear that you project when in judgment. You are the love. You are the compassion that resides within your soul.

Love will bring your species together. Love has the power to create the shifts you are looking for. Love is the way—the ultimate way out of your depressed, suppressed states.

Love will bring you closer and closer to the Divinity that you are.

The time is now to bring yourselves back to yourselves. The time is now to heal your world.

The energy of love is the answer. Love will lead the way to create the planetary shift in consciousness that you are all awaiting.

Love will raise your vibrations. Love will bring you back to yourselves and bring you all together. Love will create changes in you that will foster new tomorrows that will enhance your species, not destroy it.

There will be no war. There will be no hunger. There will be no one in wanting. There will be no cruelty. There will be no separation. There will be an understanding that you are here to support one another.

There will be no comparisons, nor competitions. There will be an understanding that you are one family, co-existing and co-creating your world in loving and compassionate ways.

There will be no blame, no regret, nor envy. There will be an understanding that you are in human form to create a fair and equitable environment for the collective.

There will be no fear, and there will be no lack of any kind. This is what is awaiting you. This is what is within your reach. This is where you are heading.

Love will penetrate wherever intention flows. Love will flow to your families, to your neighborhoods. Love will flow to your communities, to your schools, to your governments, to your businesses, to your commerce, to your nations, and to your planet. When you allow it, love will flow and transform your world.

The time is now to reclaim who you really are. You are the grace and the glory of God. The time is now to reclaim it. The time is now to embrace your true essence and begin your process of ascension.

We love you unconditionally, and lovingly penetrate the minds of those of you who are in your remembrance, infusing you with intuitive energy that will support your development. Creativity is flowing to you in the gentlest ways. Allow it to flow to you freely.

Notice your synchronicities. Trust that you are being guided. Notice the messages that are being sent to you through different forms. You are being guided. Be more open to receive this guidance.

You are not alone.

The Universe sends you messages in whatever form that resonates with you along your path of self-discovery. Be more present. Be more mindful and you will notice. These are offered you to encourage you, to inspire you, to guide you, and to remind you of our presence. You are well-supported by a higher intelligence who loves you dearly. Put aside your distractions to have this awareness.

Messages are being sent to you through your thoughts, your dreams, your feelings, ringing in your ears, goose bumps in your bodies, floral scents, cloud formations, rainbows, repeated number sequences, music, poetry, film, butterflies, birds and feathers, coins, electricity, technology. God's Divine family is always with you, nudging you, reminding you of the love and support that you have and the connection you are with your truth. There is nothing more beautiful.

Be more mindful of what you are thinking. Your thinking is keeping you in the darkest places, directly affecting your experiences.

Your memories are directly affecting your understandings. Recognize that you need to transform and transcend the direction of your memories. It is in your power to do so.

Fill your cells with the energy of the thoughts that will support you, not keep you stuck in your suffering states brought on by contracted energies of lack.

Succumb to your disharmonies and allow them to pass through you. Recognize you are not the shame, guilt, fear, grief, anger nor pride. Recognize that you can make a transference of energy by choosing differently. You can shift your vibration. There is not one of you who would willingly choose to remain in this darkness ... and you need not to.

Stored in your cellular memory remains what you allow to remain. Cleanse and clear the old. Reprogram your memory with more uplifting thought patterns. Restructure your entire inner beingness with the light and love of who you are. When you choose poorly, choose again. You came to evolve, not to go backwards. Think again.

You are the most powerful manifesters of all. You can make your lives what you wish with your choices. Along the way, you will have experiences that may not be to your liking, that you may have brought to you with others in your co-creative processes.

Learn and become better. Learn from what you experience and continue your journey as soul creators. Realize that you are ascending into greater and grander opportunities and understandings.

You are not in physicality to suffer. Release all that you are carrying. Change your thinking to change your reality, for you really are what you think. Attract what you want, not what you do not want. Be in this remembrance.

Make a conscious effort to catch yourselves and turn your thinking around when it is giving you unloving messages, recurring fear-based thoughts, creating anxiety within you. This is not who you are. This is an illusion brought about by your ego mind, the self that is not the real you.

There are many amongst you who are willing to assist you. Look around you. Opportunities for growth will come to you when you are ready. Be ready now.

Your time is now to make more positive choices to not only help yourselves but each other.

The time is now to transform your lives and get where you need to be, to live your lives more fully with meaning, excitement, and purpose, to love and respect one another with all your differences, to give each other the support that you need to further yourselves, to elevate yourselves with greater understandings, to raise your consciousness, which will allow you to live more harmoniously with one other.

As a whole—as a species in its entirety—you have lost your way. The time is now to once again find it. Your answers lie before you.

There is no need to work so hard to improve your lives. We see many of you trying—trying to get a better job, trying to attain more ... more wealth, more power, more control ... trying to meet the needs of your desires. There is no need to try. When you are vibrating at a higher frequency, there is no need to try at all. Trying is not of high vibration. Trying is a creation of the energy of fear.

All will fall into place without trying when you have positive intention and love as your driving force. One step at a time, your lives will become so much simpler and so much easier.

Life is meant to be joyful. Stop making it a struggle. There is nothing that you cannot be. There is nothing you cannot do. There is nothing you cannot have. Create fully from a place of love, with gratitude and forgiveness in your hearts.

Let go of all your hurt, all your pain, all your disappointment. Let it all go. Let go of all the darkness. Let go of old limiting beliefs about yourselves and about your world. Let go of old habits and judgments. Let them all go. Release them, as they are not serving you.

They are holding you back. They are holding you hostage. They are creating prisons within you, which block the infinite flow of Divine intelligence.

This is what is keeping your species locked in this primitive stage of development. This is what is keeping you in grade school. You are much more than you believe. Change your beliefs about yourselves to raise your vibrations, to assist with the planetary shift in consciousness that will raise you from the darkest places of your minds.

The time is now.

Awakening to the beauty of life
I go through days with wonder
Embracing the love in my heart

Spreading the joy of existence
I pass through hurdles
Like raindrops falling
Disappearing into the sunlight

Flowing with everlasting love
I shine my light
Knowing I am doing my part
In lifting the darkness

9
Life Is Meant To Be Simple

You are your own saviors.

Do not believe God will save you. God will show you the way. He will remind you that you *are* the power and you *have* the power to save yourselves. Choose to access this power and move yourselves out of your darkest states into more wonderful manifestations of your choosing.

God has sent many to show you the way. Many have led by example and are continuing to do so today. He has sent you masters of all kinds, through all walks of life.

Jesus was sent to you to remind you of who you are. He showed you the way, the way to your salvation. Jesus showed you to walk through life with compassion and love in your hearts. He came to remind you to come together and unite in the oneness of who you are. He came to remind you, as you have forgotten.

Your species has misinterpreted the teachings of Jesus. You have chosen to redirect your thinking of who you are. You have given up your responsibility as soul creators.

Christ consciousness is what will save you. Elevate your consciousness to be one with the Christ consciousness that is within you.

Do not sit in waiting—hoping God will forgive you, hoping God will save you and your world. There is no need to sit in fear and anguish. God hears you all. He sees your pain. He sees your suffering and He waits for you to find your truth. Understand you all must take responsibility. Do not sit powerless, paralyzed in fear of what your species has become and wait for others to fix your problems.

You have free will and choice to change the direction of your lives. You can heal your world. The power is within you. You have God and His Divine family on your side. This is the truth of how it is. We love you unconditionally. Absolute love is compassion and forgiveness.

There is no suffering apart from the suffering of your own choosing. Do not wait until you cross over to understand this. You have a beautiful opportunity now, while in your bodies, to create and experience fully. Do not waste this opportunity.

It is your God-given right to experience yourselves in all your completion. It is your right to be complete in the glory of who you are and to experience this fully while still in physical form. You do not need to wait.

You are forgiven. Let your past not define you. This is not who you are.

Be the best you can be. This is the reason you came, to create and experience yourselves, newer brighter and better with every decision that you make. There is no greater truth than this. There is no greater beauty. Stop punishing yourselves. You are the light. Remember this.

Be happy. Happiness is a choice. Choose happiness over despair. Happiness is a high vibration. Choose high vibrational states to help yourselves.

Bring into your experiences the joy of who you are. Create fully. This is your greatest expectation, as this is your gift—the gift of all creation.

The time is now to change how you have been living by changing how you have been thinking. Be in allowance for wonderful positive thought forms to enter. Change your thinking about who you are and where you are going. Change your thoughts to change your reality to experience the glory of who you are.

Bring yourselves out of your darkest worries and fears. Your fearful states are keeping you immobilized. These are illusions of who you are not. Release them to fully create and co-create your beautiful lives. Understand fully the unity of all in existence.

Create from your inner power—love.

Create now to fully experience your tomorrows as the love and light of who you are. There will be a transference that will bring you back to yourselves. Energy flows where intention goes. Focus on the energy you would like to produce to bring to you what you want. Keep your intentions clear and light. Flow your intentions on transmuting the darkness that resides in your world by changing the vibration that you are emanating.

The time is now.

◈

Resources will come when you are ready. Next steps will present themselves when you are ready. You have all that you need at your fingertips. Surrender to what is. Be open and be in allowance.

You are deserving, and you are all of equal value. You are one with universal energy—one with God.

◈

133

Trust and believe that you are where you need to be. Do not beat yourselves. Do not see yourselves as failures. We are here to show you the way from this point forward.

Having picked up this manual is validation that you are ready to embark on new developments.

Do not be so concerned about your past choices and experiences. Let them go to allow the energy of love and light to enter and to manifest new beautiful beginnings. The time is now.

Be patient and be in allowance. You are deserving. You are worthy. You are enough. The time is now to reclaim what is rightfully yours.

You have all come from different places with different experiences that have shaped you. You are all on different paths aiming towards the same goal. You are creating experiences that will allow you opportunity for growth.

Understand there is not one experience wasted. See the beauty of your experiences and grow through them.

Make your journey an easier one for you. Do not resist what comes. Go with the flow of life. When you are not in allowance, when you have resistance, when you find yourselves trying too hard, challenges will present themselves.

Believe that you can have what you are wanting. Trust and believe so that you are not in resistance.

Slow yourselves down. Notice minute changes within you and celebrate that which you are becoming. Take the time that you need to plant seeds of growth within you. Honour your transformation as a process that is happening from deep within you, altering the core of your entire existence.

Assist in the global transformation of your planet by doing your inner work, as you are all one unit, one family, co-existing with each other in your home, which you call planet Earth.

Notice the challenges that face you and embrace them, for they are there to bring you to the clarity that you need. Accept them. Learn from them. They are your greatest teachers. Do not anger. Do not doubt. Do not fear. Thank them, for they are presented to you to awaken you, to shift you into an alternate, more pleasing direction. Lovingly welcome and embrace them.

Look within to find your answers. Re-evaluate your choices. You will not be steered wrongly. There is no right or wrong way. Follow your heart.

Do not doubt yourselves, as doubt comes from fear. Do not live in fearful states as fear will contract your energy. Fear will disempower you. Fear will not allow the beauty of who you are to shine through.

Love is the energy that will bring you the understanding of the unity of all in existence. Fear will block you from moving forward. There is nothing to fear. You are connected to the greatest essence of all. You are connected to God. There is nothing to fear when you lovingly embrace that which you are. Do not look elsewhere. Look within to find your truth.

Focusing on others and their wrongdoings is not focusing on yourselves. It is an attempt in removing yourselves from the responsibility of your own inner growth. It is your ego mind diverting your attention onto others.

Use your focus and energy on that which is inside of you. Do not be so concerned with others and how they project themselves. Focus only on yourselves. Stop the judgment.

Others have the God essence within them just as you do. Remember this truth. They are made of the same as you. Do not be in judgment, for this will block your personal development.

Love all with their misfortunes, faults, and misgivings. Love them, for they are doing their best within their limited understandings. Bless all those around you and focus on your own personal light. Your own growth is what matters ... no one else's.

Take responsibility for your thinking patterns, words, and actions. This is your job ... no one else's. Focus only on yourselves. You all have your own personal darkness. You all have things to work on, for this is your purpose. Do not be in judgment.

Love will bring you the understanding that you need in order to reunite. Come together to transform your world. Embrace the love and light of that which you are.

Do not concern yourselves with the dysfunctions of your world. Do not place your energy on all that is frustrating you with all the injustices in your world. This will keep you stuck in your darkest states.

Change your habits. Be more conscious of what you are watching, reading and listening to. The media is not supporting you. It is suppressing you. It is satisfying your ego minds in attempts at justifying your present conditions and situations with your economies, your governments, your communities. It is feeding you falsified information to keep you in a fearful state, locked in your misery and in the control of others. Understand your media is corporate controlled and it is feeding you propaganda to keep you in an immobilized state.

Nothing will change within you when you continue to do the same. Transfer your energy into something more positive. Break this cycle of repetition. Turn off your televisions. Set aside your computers. Spend more time outdoors, absorbing all the beauty around you. Do not submit to the darkness that is projected upon you.

Change your minds to change your habits to change your world. Create the shift that will transform you and your planet. Create the shift that will transform your lives.

Your homes are filled with darkness. The energy of your televisions keep you locked in this state. Be more mindful when selecting your programs. Be more mindful with the understanding that what you watch fully impacts your psyche. What you watch plants itself deep within your cells, as it is energy. Keep your vibrations high by selecting programs that will enhance your development, not stifle it.

Choose to be in the energy of love and light.

Feed your body what it needs to support it. Listen to what soothes and comforts you. Speak with words that are gentle and kind. Meet with your friends and lovingly support each other from wherever you are. Be more mindful to help each other. This will speed up your personal process.

Be more mindful with whatever it is that you are choosing. Be more mindful to keep your vibrations high, to allow the goodness and love of who you are to enter fully into your reality.

Fill your homes with loving energy from that which you see, hear, feel, smell, taste, think, say, and do. This is what is important. Choose whatever it is that will uplift you to be the best you can be each moment of the day, for each and every moment is a new beginning. The choice is yours. Choose wisely.

Mindfulness takes practice. Lovingly accept yourselves when you fall into forgetfulness and start over. Do not be so concerned with your downfalls.

Be in remembrance that you are here to create. Create from a loving place within your hearts. Fully create from this place of lightness, for this is the only place where your suffering states will end.

Creating from a place of darkness will keep you in darkness, isolated and separate from the unity of that which you are, from each other, and from God.

Your species is much greater than this darkness that you have created on your planet. You are not of this darkness.

We are here to remind you, to be in remembrance of who you are, to bring yourselves back to yourselves. The time is now.

Change your minds and bring back your focus on what is going well in your lives and build from there. Bring your focus on all that is here and now, all the blessings, no matter how small and insignificant you may think they are. They are blessings.

Be grateful for your running water, the light of day, the roof over your heads. Focus on all that you see, hear, smell, and feel around you. This will raise your vibration. Live your lives being thankful for all that you are and all that you have, for you are all abundant.

Notice the simplicity of life. Life is meant to be simple. There are no struggles when you are in alignment. Open yourselves up to the possibilities of growth, moving forwards and upwards. You are one universal field of consciousness. Help yourselves to help each other to help your planet.

Love who you are and where you are going. Love yourselves openly and deeply, for it all starts with you. Love yourselves for who you are, with your faults and all your struggles. The time is now to make the changes that will bring you out of your struggles to embrace the love that you are more fully.

Do not look elsewhere. Do not try to find answers elsewhere. Your answers lie within. Embrace the love that is within you to experience the love that is around you.

Love yourselves to love each other, for it all starts with you.

Do not be so anxious. Do not be in despair, looking for answers. This is acting out of fear. The support that you are looking for will come to you at just the right time, when you are ready, when you are open to receive it, when you are tired and weary and willing to take the chance to let go, to give up, and to let God, the Divinity of that which you are, assist you.

Change your minds. Release your fears.

Surrender to the possibility that you are well supported, for this is the truth. Trust your answers will come to you. You will be guided. Surrender and be in allowance for this support to come to you.

The time is now.

Prepare yourselves for new beginnings. Rest more. Speak less. Focus more on what you want. Believe you can attain it. Prepare yourselves for the transformation that will change your world.

The time is now. Your world is suffering. Your planet is dying.

We are here to support you every step of the way, leading you to new beginnings, planting you with new thought forms, inspiring you with new experiences, reminding you with synchronicities, sending you messages of hope, trust, and love, uplifting you in all possible ways. Be open and be receptive. Do not be in denial.

The time is now to start your inner transformation, which will heal your world.

Trust and believe. That which you are wanting will come to you. All of what you have been waiting for will be delivered to you. One at a time, things will fall into place.

Understand the importance of working together with your energetic fields. Work with who you are. Play the game of life joyfully.

Keep your vibrations high to deliver to yourselves all your wanting. Stop your negative-thinking minds and be the best you can be by raising your vibrations. Be in deliverance, for your time is now.

Create with the compassion that you have in your hearts. Create your world the way you wish to see it. Pull yourselves together and co-create what is rightfully yours: a world filled with love, hope, and promise, a world that is peaceful, compassionate, and kind. Create the abundance that you know you are. Bring yourselves out of your discomforts.

Do not look back. Look ahead and act today to make this happen. Whatever it is that you wish to make different, to make better, is within your control, your power, to do so. It is within your reach. There is nothing that is not within reach of what you are wanting. Believe in yourself. Believe in the power that is within you, for you are the greatest creators of all.

Reclaim your power now. Believe in yourselves. Your time is now.

Do not be disillusioned by what others are doing or not doing. Focus only on yourselves, for you alone can change your world. Elevate your vibrational frequency to influence others to see their light, to begin their own transformation. Be an example. Shine the light, for when there are enough of you, this light will gloriously spread ever so quickly and change your world much more quickly.

Begin to brighten your light. Make this your focus.

The light that is within you is the light of God. This is the light of love. This is the energy of all creation, and this is the energy that can bring you back to yourselves. This is the energy that will bring balance back to your planet, for this is the most powerful energy of all.

Love who you are and know that you are the love of Divine creation. There is nothing more beautiful. You are Divine perfection. The time is now to remember this, as you have forgotten.

Your planet needs you. It is in a suffering state with all the suffering of your species. Your energy is not supporting you. Your energy is breaking the core existence of your species. Understand the impact this has on you. It is destroying you. There is little humanness left in humanity. This is not who you are.

Hold the intention of vibrating in a peaceful, grateful state, to help yourselves—to heal and balance your planet. Be in this remembrance when you wake in the morning and when go to bed at night. Go about your day in this remembrance.

Change your thoughts to be in alignment with who you are. Be more mindful of what you are thinking. This is destroying you.

Live in the truth of who you are, with the love that you have to offer to each other. Love yourselves and your neighbor.

Love will bring you all together. Love is the most powerful expansive energy of all.

Love will gloriously spread and joyously bring you back to the unity and harmony of that which you are.

Love will bring you all together in co-existence with each other, transforming the fabric of your creations, transmuting them into the light of the Divine. Love will bring magnificent manifestations with every decision that you make, with experiences that unite you all, not separate you.

Love is a power like no other. Love will bring down your barriers.

You reflect what you see before you. You affect everyone around you. Do not believe your thoughts and your actions have no impact on your world. They do, and they do at a great level. You affect one another, and you affect your planet. You affect your universe. Every one of you matters in the cosmos of the universe. You matter, and you affect your world either positively or negatively in its entirety.

What you are experiencing today in your world is the ultimate result of what your species has created.

All of the imbalances of your planet, all of the environmental catastrophes, all the madness of destructive patterning and distorted beliefs, hopelessness and desperation, poor health, and lack of concern for your environment, corruption and greed, conflict and inequality, chaos from personal to global ... are all in line with, and a result of, the vibrational frequency that you as a species have been emanating. It is an energy that is keeping you in a suppressed state. You are creating your lives from your lower selves—your ego.

We are here to remind you again this is not serving you. This is not serving your planet. It is making both you and your home sick. It is affecting your mental, emotional, physical, and spiritual states. It is affecting the balance of your planet.

The role that you are playing in all of creation is a vital one—one that impacts your entire existence as a species. You alone can destroy, just as you alone can rebuild. Stop continuing to destroy. You are not your ego. You are much greater.

You are the love and light of All That Is, the Source of all creation. You are made of the God essence that is within you. This is who you are.

The time is now to take responsibility for this noble, humbling understanding of who you are, and begin the new process of bountiful creations.

Love yourselves, for this is where it all begins.

It starts with loving yourself. The love that you have for yourselves will grow and spread. It is that powerful. Love yourselves like no other. The rest will take care of itself. It all starts with you and your own personal vibration.

Manifest tomorrows that bring you joy, to enhance the love that is within you.

Your soul is reaching out wanting ever so graciously for you to drop all the self-doubt, the insecurities, the judgments, and the uncertainties that you have placed upon yourselves. Your soul would love for you to focus on all the wonder of who you are and your purpose of evolution.

Love yourselves like no other. Do not sit in judgment, waiting for things to change to begin your process. Look in the mirror. Look into your eyes and affirm to yourselves the love that you have for yourselves. Affirm this daily to believe it, for you have forgotten. You will see who you really are when you look into your eyes. You will see your soul essence, the beauty and unconditional love that you are and the love that you have for all. You will remember.

"I love myself. I love my life. I love who I am. I am love." Repeat this to believe it. It all starts with you.

Painful memories gently slipping away
Opening the door
To the wonder
Of who I am

10
Break Free From Limitation

Be prepared as you will face challenges. Be patient for this is a journey of self-exploration and growth. Practice non-judgment. Stay focused and be in remembrance of the power that you are.

Be proud of your achievements and glorify the progress that you are making each day. Never look upon yourselves as failures. You are nothing short of miracles, each one of you.

Manifest from the beauty that you are and unify the love that you have for each other. Live in this truth and abundance will flow. Align yourselves with your true essence. The time is now.

A great global shift in consciousness is awaiting you. Your planet is undergoing an awakening. Many are feeling this. You are awakening to the understanding that you are much, much more, to the understanding that there is much, much more, to the understanding that there is more to life, to death, to God, than your limiting beliefs and what your minds are telling you.

Many of you are awakening to your highest potentiality, living in a more conscious state, seeing more clearly now. This is the beautiful reality.

Re-align your thinking to create your own inner shift. Awaken to the truth of who you are.

Create the abundant life that you are longing for and so deserve. Anchor in your highest self.

Your home needs you. Assist your planet in the shift that will bring back the balance that it so desperately needs. Live your lives more peacefully. The chaos that your species has created is not who you are.

Begin by bringing your own inner state into balance. Find your own peace and extend this joyful state outward to all around you, to your families, to your communities, to your governments, to your entire planet and universe. It all starts with you and your personal energy frequency. Do not look elsewhere for answers.

Join forces with those who can see more clearly. You have incarnated to assist each other as this is the way—the way to the opening of your third eye, to see more clearly, to attain deeper truths and understandings, to create more fully from a place of clarity.

Lead by example. Begin your transformative process now. You are one with universal Source energy—one with God.

Be more aware of organized groups that you are choosing. Be more aware that there are many that limit you that identify you with that which you are not. Choose to join with groups that allow for your expansion.

Remove yourselves from settings that keep you locked in your miseries that keep you feeding from others that are experiencing the same depressed states. You are not this doom and gloom. You are not this sadness. This energy is of low vibration. Choose wisely.

Know in your hearts that you will get past the pain and the suffering. Find the strength that is built within you to surpass these "e-motions," for this is what they are: energy in motion. Allow them to filter through you and transmute into the light. You are not your pain. You are not your suffering. You are much greater.

Do your work to surpass your traumas. Feel your fears to process and release them. Allow yourselves the support that you need.

Do not replay scenarios of your past. Do not keep your traumas alive. Replaying your past does not reinforce your development. It stagnates your growth.

Start the process of your own development. Follow your inner guidance to take you where you need to be. Your gut instinct will take you there. Do not second guess the first and foremost intuition you have. This is your soul speaking to you. This is God speaking to you. Follow your own inner guidance system. You all have this. Access it now.

The more you slow yourselves down, the more you take the time to breathe consciously, the more you pay attention, the sooner you will hear. Inspiration will come and guidance ... you shall receive. Your soul is speaking to you. Listen.

Your angels are supporting you. Ask for their assistance. You have abundant support. Remember this. You are not alone. You are never alone. Have the courage to break free from your suffering states. Have the courage to surrender. Have the courage to awaken to who you truly are.

Acceptance is the key. Acceptance will set you free.

Your pain is no different from others. You have all experienced pain in one form or another. There is not one pain greater than the other. It is in one's own perception of their experiences.

Your pain has served its purpose for your personal growth.

Support groups that deal with addictions are worthy. They are in place to help those who believe they cannot help themselves. Believe you can.

Do not believe you have an addiction. Do not affirm to yourselves that you have an addiction, as this is not serving you. This is blocking you. Your compulsive-thinking mind is ruling you, making you believe you are not worthy. Control your mind so it doesn't control you. This is the key. Addiction proves your loss of control.

Regain your power by regaining control of your mind. Understand completely that you are not your mind. You are much greater. You are not the addiction. This is your past. Break free from your past. You are worthy, and you are greatness. Believe this to create the shift in your consciousness that will set you free.

Choose your groups wisely. Do they elevate you? Do they inspire you? Choose wisely.

Do not see yourselves as failures. You are not. Your experiences are worthy, as they have opened your eyes to new possibilities. Your experiences have allowed you to grow and become more complete in the perfection of who you are.

Do not keep revisiting your past. Whatever happened served its purpose for your spiritual growth by your agreement. Whatever you did to get to where you are today is perfection. See yourselves as Divine perfection, and from this place create—create new beginnings.

You are worthy. You are abundant, and you have all that you need to access the wonders of the universe. Take back your power. Reclaim who you are. Affirm to yourselves the magnitude of your potentiality. You are greatness: Divine perfection. This is who you are. Remember this.

Go within. This is the greater assistance that you are looking for. Access the power that you have within you, built inside of you, for this is your true power. This is where you will find the strength you are looking for to break free. You are worthy. You are not your addiction.

Affirm the power that you are. "I am greatness. I am worthy. I am perfection. I am an extension of God."

Repeat this to believe it, for this is who you are. Convince yourselves, for you have forgotten.

Meditate to find your peace. Look for the Divine in you. Meditation and prayer will get you there. There is no greater way.

Ask to receive. Ask with an open heart in humble gratitude. Ask. God is listening. Sit in silence, close your eyes, and gently ask. This is how you pray. This is how you talk to God.

Do not plead for guidance. Do not beg for forgiveness. You are all guided. You are all forgiven. God is not vengeful. God understands each one of you. God is compassion. God is the light.

Do not shed tears. There is no need. God hears and answers all your prayers. Go deep within and ask with an open heart. Find your peace and ask ... and then listen.

We see that many of you are choosing to remain in your suffering states. We see that you are punishing yourselves with mistakes you believe you have made. We want to remind you that you are not helping yourselves or anyone when you remain in this pain. You are keeping yourselves locked in guilt and regret.

Choose differently. Pull yourselves out of your pain. Choose to see yourselves as the brightest stars that you are. Choose to live your lives fully, for you only have one in this lifetime.

You are Source energy in physical form, having incarnated to bring about experiences to advance yourselves. The time is now to reflect and ask yourselves if this indeed is what you have been doing.

Know in your hearts the pain and the suffering that you are undergoing has not gone unnoticed. We are always with you, supporting you, comforting you, wiping your tears. We are grieving with you. Our hearts are heavy when your hearts are heavy. We love you and want you to know that we are just as much affected by the turmoil in your world.

We, in the higher realms of existence, in the non-physical world, are not separate from you. We see you. We feel you. We are here for you. We understand you. We love you.

We know you do not want this. We know that you want peace. We know that you want abundance. We know that you want love. We are here to remind you that you can have this. You can have it all.

The time is now.

Religion was once a beautiful reality. It brought people together joyfully. It created community. People worshipped the God of their choosing and this kept them focused on being the best they could be, living in the truth of who they were.

Over time, greed and manipulation took reign as religion administered falsehoods, adhering to what humanity is not, in their attempts to control the masses. Fear-based tactics were used to suppress their communities.

With more and more power and control, these systems built within them false realities that only benefited the few, not the collective. With fewer and fewer members, they did what they could to instill fear to make believers out of the nonbelievers, introducing various methods of dominance. Bigger truths were withheld. Power and suppression were the focus and has thus remained.

Judgment, competition, and greed permeate through your religions with manipulation and distortion of the truth ... the true word of God. These organized units of control keep their members in the belief that you are separate. This is not the truth of who you are.

From the beginning of time, religion has played its role in creating barriers amongst you, causing strife, causing battle, creating grievances that separate you. There has never been agreement. There has never been unity.

The progress of your planet has been slow and arduous with these beliefs that have stemmed largely from your organized units of control. They serve their own but discriminate others. Their beliefs are distorted. They believe this is what God wants.

Please know that we understand you are doing the best you can with what you know. We see this, and we commend you for trying—trying to be the best you can be. There is so much more you do not know. We encourage you to be open to exploration for expansion.

The time has come to re-evaluate your institutions, your societies, your communities, and your governments. The time has come to question whether they have served their purpose. You must question. You must take the time to think for yourselves and question.

Do not follow what others are telling you. Others are telling you what they believe to be true with their own limiting beliefs, in accordance with their upbringings and biases, with what they have been told and with what they see to be true through their own eyes.

There is so much more. The time has come to be more open and welcoming of newer truths, bigger truths, truths that we are putting before you now.

Slow yourselves down and reflect on what you see. Decide for yourselves if life has improved for your world with organized units of control. Take the time to think and reflect.

Have your faiths brought love? Have they encouraged unity? Have they fostered growth? Have they encouraged you to question, to explore, to create, to be fearless, to be yourselves?

Or have your faiths suppressed you, blocked you from your intuitive connection? Have they instilled fear in you—fear of not doing the right thing, of not acting the right way? Have they reminded you of your imperfections?

There is no need to fear. God is love—absolute love, infinite love. God loves you all with all your perceived imperfections.

God is forgiveness. God is compassion. God is unity. There is nothing God wants or needs from you.

You are here to create and to experience. You are here to grow and develop. You are in physicality to mature, to expand. You are not here to regress.

Have your faiths brought people together? You must reflect and you must question.

Your religions have not encouraged love. They have not fostered infinite love for humanity, for all of you, when they speak of redemption, when they speak of a God that is unforgiving, when they speak of a God that wants and needs you to behave a certain way, when they put limitations on you. This is not what love is.

They have not encouraged love when they choose to separate and discriminate and divide, when they choose to shame, blame, and inject terrible punishments on you, when they make you believe you are less than. This is not love.

Love has no borders. Love has no boundaries. Love is infinite and love is unconditional. This is what love is.

Your religions have made you believe you are unworthy. They have set limitations on you.

Understand that there is no one faith greater than the other, as you have so wrongly been made to believe. Your faith is not the ultimate faith, surpassing all others. Your religions have divided you, making you into something you are not, creating judgments within you.

This is creating confusion. This is creating fear—fear that you need to be in the right faith and you need to do the right things to have salvation, to be accepted by God into His kingdom. You are living in fear, which is suppressing the creative intelligence of who you are.

Your faiths have misinterpreted God's teachings.

Stop this delusion. Wake up people.

No one is going to hell.

There is no hell, regardless of what you have been led to believe. Hell is a state, not a place. The hell that is a reality is the hell of your own choosing, experiencing it through your own creations in this lifetime. It is you choosing to be in this state, choosing it subconsciously.

God sees you as the light and the love of His creations. You are His children. You are brothers and sisters. It is only when you see yourselves in this way that your beliefs about yourselves will shift.

Your religions have manipulated their power and have created codependency.

This is not what God is. God is love without restrictions in your personal freedom. There is no one way to heaven ... to the peace of that which you are. There are many. God loves you all and accepts you all as you are.

Break down your barriers and unite in the oneness that you are. You are living in one global community all having different experiences but all wanting the same. Unite as the community that you are. See yourselves as the family that you are. You are all wanting the same.... peace, love and harmony.

There is competition amongst you. There is no one greater than the other. Believe this to access it. Stop your competitions in your homes, playgrounds, schools, governments, nations, and businesses. Stop trying to prove your worth. This is creating animosity, jealousy, judgment, intolerance, hatred for one another. Stop your competitions.

See yourselves as equals. Rejoice and celebrate your differences. You all have gifts and talents. Celebrate your uniqueness.

More and more are coming to deeper understandings as you are awakening. You are ascending into higher consciousness, understanding more, attaining more wisdom. This is a beautiful reality.

Search and you shall find. Question and be open to receive. The walls that separate you are becoming thinner and thinner. There is great hope.

Those who preach separation do not believe in unity. They are lost. They are bitter. They are unforgiving. They are holding onto who you are not. They blame and they shame.

There is no one greater than the other. You are all going through the process of life. You are evolving each at your own pace, whatever you allow.

The time is now to help each other. Understand that your world is not functioning effectively. Your world is in crisis. There is global dysfunction. There is something missing in your understandings. Assist each other by accelerating your own personal growth.

Spread the love, dear ones. Spread the love and the light of that which you are. Open yourselves up to broader understandings. Allow the love that you are to flow through you.

More and more universal places of love and worship are bringing more and more people together. This is a beautiful remembrance that there is hope. More and more places are opening their doors to all, regardless of creed, color, gender, culture, or background. This is a wonderful reality amongst you.

There is great hope to unite in oneness. There is great hope to release all your doubts and insecurities. There is always hope, as there is impermanence. There is nothing that cannot change. Life is impermanent. You are never stuck. This is a beautiful reality.

The division amongst you is very deep and bitter. There is hostility, anguish, and cruelty amongst you. Operating at this level further stabilizes your truth as you know it now. This is not who you are.

Understand you are all special in your own uniqueness. You are soul imprints, each with your own energetic make-up. You carry with you many lifetimes of experiences.

You are different from one another, but you are not separate. Do not isolate yourselves. Look upon each other as equals, each carrying lifetimes of wisdom, knowledge, and expertise. All is waiting to surface. Allow it to come forth. Bring it forward, as this is who you are.

This belief of separation is keeping you stuck and immobile. This is not how it is. This is not the truth of God. It is time to think more deeply about what you have chosen and choose again.

Begin to question. Begin to question. Do not follow like sheep. Your holy books have served their purpose. It is time now to understand that your holy books are not complete. There is so much more that you do not know. We are here to help you with these understandings, these deeper truths about life and about God.

See more clearly now. Be more open to new understandings. Admit to yourselves that there is more than what you have been told and believe to know. Your holy scriptures are incomplete in their entireties.

New understandings have been presented to you many, many times, time and time again. Re-evaluate and open to these new possibilities.

Your world is not functioning effectively. It is merely in existence.

There is no greater time than now to open to new insights, possibilities, and opportunities ... to open the door to heightened awareness.

As with all of life, religion needs to evolve. It needs to evolve as humanity evolves. Everything by design is meant to evolve. The problem lies herein.

Your religions, based on their sets of principles interpreted from their holy books, have remained as they were, immobilized since the beginning of time. They have not been allowed growth. They have blocked new understandings. They remain with the beliefs of the middle ages. This is creating chaos in your world.

With the evolution of humanity, with the growth of your species, with new and wonderful advancements in science, technology, and medicine, you must wonder why then has religion remained stagnant? Why? Contemplate. Ask yourselves. Dare to ask.

The time is now to understand more completely. Holy scriptures came about from channeled messages—Divine messages of God. They were deeply accepted and followed, as the true word of God, often misinterpreted, but followed. They were not questioned. They were revered as the way it is and the way to please God.

Humanity believed, as many of you today, that God is outside you. They personified God. They believed that He was watching over them, with a watchful eye, patiently waiting for them to improve themselves. They believed that He was somewhere out there—up there. They believed that they were here, and God was there. They believed that God was not a part of them.

This belief was and still is one of the biggest misconceptions of all. Many of you believe this fallacy. Understand that God is consciousness.

Elevate your consciousness to feel the God essence within you. Elevate yourselves to be one with God and create the world that you are all longing for from this place of oneness.

God is consciousness—universal consciousness. We shall continue referring to this highest intelligence as "God" and as a "He" as this is what we see is most comfortable to you.

Understand that God is within and around everyone and everything. He is not separate from you.

People believed and still believe in a vengeful God, a God who places rules of conduct before you, a God who needs to challenge you to determine whether you are worthy enough to join Him in everlasting peace. This is not the truth. This is not the truth at all.

Your holy books have been written again and again, falsified with human understandings, which have served to keep order of community. They are not the concrete word of God.

There is no need to follow any version. There is no need to try to understand these texts. There is a need to understand fully that you are love and you are loved, wherever you are on this journey of life, with all that has been presented to you, with all the challenges you are facing, with all the heartache, with all the pain. You are accepted. You are forgiven. You are never criticized, never judged.

Your purpose is to grow, develop, and evolve. Your purpose is to become expansive. God has given you free will. Choose to move forward with these new understandings. Question, for it is only when you dare to question, that your beliefs begin to shift to new directions.

Do not live in fear. You have done nothing wrong.

The global challenges that you are facing today are not challenges that can be rectified at the physical level. Open your minds and connect to your hearts to allow for growth. Your species is at a stalemate. You have not been kind to each other. Your world is in a state of dysfunction.

You are most deserving of peace, harmony, and joy. You are most worthy of all that you wish for. There is not one of you who is not deserving, no matter where you have been or what you have done. God is light. God is unconditional love. God is forgiveness.

Your beliefs about yourselves have stagnated your growth. You are most worthy of attaining wisdom and glorified Divine truths.

The time is now.

Open to deeper understandings. Believe you are worthy of downloading God's messages. There are many amongst you today that channel the energy of the higher realms of existence. There are many in communication with non-physical beings. Believe this, as this is the truth. We are not separate from you. We are oneness connected to the universal energy of all creation, to God.

Do not denounce. Do not dismiss those who are bringing forth profound insight, those who are giving you hope. Do not judge those who are giving you greater understandings.

They have been sent to you to show you the way. They are selflessly working with you to inspire you, to assist you in coming into your own truth. They are here to tell you the truth. Be more open to understand what you have yet to understand. Follow your hearts.

Your religions believe in the limitations of humanity. They believe there can never be anyone worthy enough in this day and age to attain higher wisdom. This is closing the window of opportunity for growth.

Your faiths do not want you to question. They do not want you to challenge. They believe in humanity's unworthiness. Your religions have fostered fear amongst you. This is not the truth of who you are.

Trust and believe you are here to question. Look within your hearts to find your answers. Those who preach are following what has been the truth for thousands of years. This is not the truth of God. God urges you to find your freedom once again. He urges you to break free from those who are holding you back. God wants you to find your peace, to think for yourselves, and trust what is in your hearts.

Your holy books have done more damage than you know. Courageously move away and know you are on the path towards your salvation, the salvation you are looking for, the salvation that will once again bring you all together, in peace and in harmony.

Look around. Where is your species now? Is there peace amongst you? Is there harmony?

You are living in a world where there is hatred, greed, and dysfunction. You are treating each other in the most inhumane ways.

Your species is not one with your true nature. You are not in alignment with God.

The time is now to reflect on how you are living.

There is inequity, hatred, violence, greed, and despair in your world. Your species is divided. Your beliefs are creating tremendous imbalances in your home.

The time is now to change your minds. Understand completely that you are not different than others. Your nation is not better than others. Your culture is not greater. Your ideology is not the ultimate ideology.

You have separated yourselves for fear of losing control. Remove this fearful state. You are not helping yourselves by removing yourselves from others. You are creating divisions, and this is keeping you stuck in a false reality—a reality of that which you are not.

This is not the truth of how it is. We are here to awaken you. This is not how life works. You are not living fully when living in this state. You are not in alignment with God's truth. You are creating your tomorrows from a place of limitation and resistance. This is not who you are.

Break down the barriers that separate you. Open your hearts to each other. Help one another to see the Divine perfection of who you are. Understand that your institutions are not serving you. They are keeping you under their control. Understand that your holy books are not complete. There is misinterpretation and wisdom that is missing.

Wake up. Think for yourselves. You have forgotten. Do not follow those who believe in separation, who talk about removing themselves to protect themselves.

Protection comes when you are in alignment with God's truth. You are protected. Bring yourselves back into alignment. Stop hurting each other. Stop believing you are greater than the other. You all have your own individuality, with your gifts and talents, which must be celebrated. Celebrate your differences with the understanding that you are all wonderful with your own uniqueness. You all have something to offer to your world.

The time is now to break down your barriers and reunite in the oneness of that which you are.

Save yourselves to save your planet. Heal your world.

Do not condemn others for their choices. Do not condemn yourselves. The time is now to awaken and consciously accelerate your evolutionary process. Make better choices. Change your thinking. Open to new ideas. Celebrate your becoming. Create the shift that is awaiting you. Live in the truth of who you are.

Choose to be in alignment. Follow your inner guidance. Awaken to the peace that lies within.

Remember that you are the light. You are of God essence. You are in physical form to create and to experience ... to evolve ... not to retract. We are here to remind you, for you have forgotten. Take back your power with this remembrance.

Your planet needs your assistance. It is of vital importance that more of you understand this to assist in elevating the consciousness of the collective.

We are planting seeds of inspiration within you. We are encouraging you to see more clearly. We are assisting you in lifting yourselves out of your darkest states, in seeing the light of who you really are.

Raise your vibrations to elevate your consciousness.

The time is now to pay more attention to how you are living. We challenge you to take one day and record your feelings throughout your day. Record how you are feeling from morning to night. Take the time to take more notice.

Take a chance to see where you are as an exercise of self-love. Take this opportunity to examine yourselves to fully understand yourselves.

Practice being more aware of the vibration you are transmitting. This will be an awakening.

Are you vibrating high through the energy of love? Are you fostering kindness, compassion, patience, acceptance, generosity or are you vibrating low through the energy of fear fostering intolerance, judgment, blame, shame, anger.

Slow yourselves down and take more notice how you are feeling with what you are feeding your bodies and your minds.

Notice your choice of words. Notice how you are communicating. What are you listening to? What are you watching? Reading? What are you drinking? What are you eating? Notice how you are feeling with all that you are doing when with your families, friends, colleagues, pets, and wherever you are throughout your day.

And more importantly, notice where your mind is taking you. Take more notice and record.

How you are feeling throughout your day is your personal energy frequency speaking to you.

Record all your day fully. Reflect on your findings. Think more deeply on how you are living. Everything holds a vibration. Take responsibility for your personal state, as this is what is leading your life and also impacting the collective. Choose wisely for all is energy, and it is either supporting you or weighing heavily upon you.

The time is now to examine and fully understand where you are on your evolutionary scale and consciously make adjustments.

Be in remembrance to create opportunities to feel your greatest, as this is the energy you want to anchor and support to manifest the reality of your choosing.

Choose wisely what you are fueling your bodies and your minds.

The time is now to understand deeper truths, to live more completely, more peacefully, more joyfully in an abundant state whereby creativity will forever flow to you and shape your realities.

Be in allowance for miracles. Be in allowance to be the magnet of your desires.

Choose to speak with integrity. Speak gently. Speak lovingly. Notice the beauty around you. Observe the glory that surrounds you.

Slow down long enough to appreciate your moments. Lovingly express gratitude to open your hearts. Slow down and feel. Take the time to feel and appreciate. You have so much. See and feel what you have and be thankful to manifest more.

Take the time to be with yourselves. Sit in solitude. Love your silence. Embrace the peace that you are. It is through prayer and meditation that you can find this. Wisdom will flow. Give your mind what it needs to grow—to cleanse, and to clear residual negativity, lowering vibration, that which does not serve you. Be open for love to enter, for this is who you are.

Take the time to be with yourselves, to awaken to your highest potentiality. God is listening. God is here for you. He has not forgotten you.

Thank your planet, for this is your home. Thank Mother Earth daily for supporting you. Give her the vibration of love that she needs to assist her in her healing. Spend more time with her. Feel her vibration. Spend more time outdoors.

Feed your mind, body, and soul all that it needs to grow, develop, and evolve.

You are important—more important than you know. You matter, as there is no other like you. Love yourselves. It all starts with you. Break away from the patterns of limitation to access the infinite intelligence of who you really are. Your species is missing the glory of life—the glory of living fully with a body and a mind. You are not in physicality to live in despair. You have incarnated to live your lives completely, to live freely without stipulations and regulations.

The time is now to stop putting up barriers, fortifying blockages and resistance. Allow the greatness that you are to surface, for it has been dormant far too long. Use your free will to access this now.

Mysteries of the Universe
Unfolding ever so brightly
Calling out for notice

11
Live In Alignment

Infinite resources are available to you. There is enough for all. There is more than enough. Come to this understanding. Do not believe those who are telling you otherwise.

What you have been led to believe is not the truth. It is falsified information to keep you in a suppressed state, in a state of forgetfulness. This has contributed to the loss of your personal power. You have given it up—given it to others.

Use your free will to open to your highest intelligence. Use your soul intelligence for scientific advancements. This is where your power is. Operate from your higher selves. Your minds can only take you thus far.

Understand that your corporate powers are no wiser than you. They are manipulating the power that you have given them for personal gain and profit. They are not wiser, better, more knowledgeable than you.

They are suppressing your intuitive intelligence by feeding you sick produce. They are ruining your food supply, and they are polluting your waters.

Wake up people. Take back your power. Do not trust those who separate you. Do not allow others to control you.

Choose to bring yourselves back to the truth of who you are, to create the shift in power you have been waiting for. Wake up and begin your process of development.

The time is now.

Return yourselves back to yourselves. We love you and are encouraging you. You are not alone. We are here to inspire you. We see much more than you. We are here to help you. We are sending you all that you need to assist you in your awakening.

Your monetary system is not helping you. It has created imbalance within you. The rich are getting richer and the poor poorer. This is how your system works. The more you have, the more you want. Greed feeds your existence, not love for one another. Mismanagement of your finances supports your dysfunction.

Break down your barriers to live more fully. Think more clearly to understand more fully. Money will not save you. Money will destroy you.

Understand you are the manifesters of your realities. You have control of your lives and you have the power to alter your realities. What you create and co-create play out as you create them.

It is time to understand you must lead your lives with your hearts, not within the limitations set before you by your minds. This is where your power is.

Trust in the new beginnings that are created daily, with more and more in understanding of deeper truths. The shift is happening now. Feel it, as it is here.

More and more are opening your hearts to greater insight. More and more are opening your minds to the glory of unification, peace, and harmony for all.

Hold the intention of elevating your consciousness to come out of your darkness. Heighten your awareness. Increase your ability to grasp new concepts and opportunities. Activate your own personal transformative process. The choice is yours.

With each day, you are getting closer and closer to the inner truth of who you are. You are moving into broader perspectives. We are so very pleased.

There is no need for suffering. There is no need for mental, emotional, nor physical disharmony and dysfunction. You can transform out of these false perceptions of who you are.

Too much emphasis is placed on what is not working for you. You are too much in your minds. There is not one different than the other. There is not one that has the fate of any disease or disorder. It is all in your fabrications. The disease, the disorder, is in your minds.

Your minds are playing tricks, making you believe that you are prone to one imbalance or another in accordance with your families' histories, in accordance with your DNA. You are listening to falsified information coming from systems who wish to disempower you. You are listening to those who are playing God.

There is no greater wrong than this. You are allowing yourselves to believe you are less than.

Understand there are no victims. There are never any victims but the limited states of your own choosing.

Understand it is in your power to activate your genes to produce the results that you are seeking. It is in your power to wake them from their dormancy states by feeding them what they need. Understand your environments play a great role in how you are functioning internally. Your diets play a vast role as do your thoughts, words and actions. Feed your genes what is of high vibration to awaken them to the light. You are not destined to any disharmony—that of the mind or of the body. Believe you can redirect your supposed fate. You can heal yourselves.

You are making yourselves believe you are disabled.

Realize your minds and your bodies are malfunctioning because you are feeding them poorly. Take notice and make more conscious choices in how you are functioning.

There is no need for any part of you to malfunction. You are not meant to break down. You are meant to have a physical experience, in optimal condition, for as long as you wish.

We see many of your species taking medications to combat the stresses you have put on your bodies and on your minds. Have more awareness that your medications are keeping you stuck.
Medication slows you down. It distorts your thinking and keeps you at a place of no desire. There is no creativity in this state. You are alive, but you are not living fully. You cannot dream. You cannot create from this place. You are at a stalemate.

Take more care to be the best you can be. Live to your highest potentiality. Take better care of your bodies. Take better care of your minds.

Stop your medications and take back your power. Wean yourselves from such poisons. It is critical. With the assistance of professionals, the chemical imbalances in your brains can be altered and balanced. Trust in natural practices. Do not trust those who are promoting chemicals. Do not feed into the pharmaceutical industries, as they are here to destroy you. Money is their sole interest, making more, nothing else.

Believe more in yourselves. You have the power to heal yourselves. Go within. Meditate, pray, trust, and believe that you are the ultimate power. Trust that you are protected. You are guided.

You are loved. You have an entire crew working with you, assisting you on your journey through life. God's Divine family of guardians, spirit guides, angels, archangels, and ascended masters are here with you, supporting you. Realize this, as this is the truth. Realize this to access it.

Live with gratitude in your hearts, for you have so much already. It is you who has manifested what you have before you. Celebrate your accomplishments. Celebrate your lives and create more with awareness living in the present moment, without stress, and without anxiety.

There are too many of you who are suffering. We feel your pain. There is no need for such sorrow. You are much greater. Rejoice in who you are. Remember your greatness, as you have forgotten.

Trust the light within you. Light your flame. Activate your greatness.

Feel the light. It is there within each one of you. Go within to feel. Access it now.

Be in this remembrance to heal.

Look within to find your answers. Look within and you will find what you are looking for. Sit in stillness. Your answers are there.

Your species has lost itself in the complexity of your materialistic world. Where are you? Who are you? Ask yourselves. Where are you ... in your minds, in your hearts? Who are you really? Why are you here? Where is your focus? What are you putting your energy into ... into the development of your ego self or into the development of your heart-centered soul self?

Understand fully you are in control of your reality. Understand your mind will keep you in your suffering states while your heart will free you ... free you from worry, doubt, anger, criticism—all forms of fear. Ask yourselves where you are now. Ask yourselves.

Is this what you really want? Are you happy? Are you at peace?

How you wish to live your lives is your choice. We are here to encourage you. We love you and encourage you to choose the path that will lead you to the end of your suffering, the end of your egoic competitive states and into new beginnings—beginnings of the love that you are and the love that you have for yourselves and for your world. You are interconnected. You are oneness. Choose to see yourselves as that.

Unite as one. Come together with the understanding that you can create a new world that is free from your negative states. The choice is yours, and it all starts with you.

Together you will create a bountiful world. There will be no more pain. Pain is self-created. There will be harmony. This is who you are.

Believe in yourselves to manifest your desires. Your insecurities are blocking you from acquiring all your wants. Your beliefs are blocking your progress. Understand this as the truth.

Use all your senses to attract whatever it is that you are wanting. The more you believe, the greater and faster the universe will deliver. With faith and trust, you can create whatever you wish. You are that powerful. Believe in this truth as the truth of All That Is.

You are one universal energy connected to greater energies of higher realms. We are all connected. We work together in the deliverance of your desires. We are here to assist you.

The time is now to understand deeper truths, to help yourselves and bring about the transformation that your planet needs. The time is now to create the shift that will bring back the balance that your planet needs, one that will harmonize the interconnected energies.

Understand that changing your circumstances, physical or emotional states at the physical level is arduous. Surrender to create shifts at the energetic level. This is where real change begins, when you are in alignment with the Source that created you.

Allow yourselves to experience the light and love of who you are, and the power you have, to heal yourselves. Acceptance, forgiveness and gratitude will take you there. Allow God to work through you. You are here to create a wonderful world, to experience the joy of living in your bodies. Understand this fully. You are not meant to suffer.

Release all your fears, your insecurities, your lack of self-worth. This is not who you are. No one will care for you as much as you may care for yourselves. Love yourselves. Remember this. You must come first, not your children, not your spouse, not your parents, not your friends. Open your arms and embrace the love that you are. Accept yourselves and move forward. It all starts with you.

Attract what you want in your lives. Live fully and create from a place of trust, not from a place of doubt and uncertainty. There is nothing you cannot bring into your experiences. Be confident and know that you are the greatest creators. You have the grandest potentialities.

You are in absolute control of your lives with your thoughts and emotions, with your own personal vibration. Be in alignment with the energies that support you. Be in alignment with God.

Accept yourselves to accept others. Do not be in judgment. Live with love in your hearts.

Come together. Unite in oneness, for this is who you are. Assist each other in your evolutionary processes.

Be the patience. Be the acceptance. Be the forgiveness. Be the kindness. Be more loving to one another. Be that which you wish for yourselves. Only then may you fully experience this.

Speak with love in your hearts, remembering the beauty of who you are. Help each other to help yourselves. You all affect each other. You are in existence with the universal energies that interconnect you.

Understand fully your planet vibrates solely on the energy that you emanate. The amplification of your collective energy creates the energy of your world. Your energetic fields merge and create global energies.

Your countries are divided. The energetic patterns are not evenly distributed.

Raise your vibrations to assist your masses—those who are in continual pain and suffering. Help them out of their despair. They are feeding off of the illusion of lack. Be of assistance. Help yourselves to help others. You are one family. You have one home. See yourselves working together in peace and in harmony. Unite in this oneness.

Break the cycle of fear and separation. Change your minds to change your vibrations to change your realities. There is enough for everyone on your planet. There is no need for suffering. Create the shift that will bring about the transformation that your planet needs.

Change your views. Change your beliefs. This will alter your outlook and create new opportunities that will bring forth new developments. Access the soul intelligence that you are.

The time is now to transform the vibration of your planet, to lift it up, to help all who are paralyzed in their suffering states, to lift them up to a heightened awareness that will transform everything.

The time is now to heal your world. .

Be in this remembrance. You are most worthy. Allow the love, light, and compassion that you are to flourish. Bring it forth, for only you can access what is rightfully yours.

Your world needs you to be in this remembrance. Your species has forgotten that you are one unified human collective, with the essence of purity ... of God.

We are here to remind you. Access love now.

Let go of the past—the judgments, the criticism of yourselves and others, the blame, the shame, the guilt, the doubt. Let go of all of what is painful, for all of this is keeping you from experiencing the greatness that you are.

Live your lives with laughter. Live fully. Live a playful existence. Do not be so serious. Do not allow yourselves to get immersed in self-righteousness. Enjoy life. That's what it is meant for. Love who you are.

Live your lives connected to your hearts. All will come to you— all of what you wish for. You are here to have it all.

Be in remembrance you are having a human experience for expansion—expansion of your consciousness. You are here to come to higher, more elevated understandings about who you are and where you fit in. You are here to elevate to new heights of awareness whereby you may come to fully know and understand yourselves and the unity of all in existence.

Remember the light that you are and look for the light in others. Encourage others. Speak with kindness. Speak with love in your hearts. Shine your light. Be in this remembrance.

Be more accepting. Release your judgments. Allow others to come into their own remembrances and understandings.

Feel the vibration of peace. Feel the vibration of love.

Shine brightly, sweet ones. Shine brightly and transform your world. It is the energy of love that will bring you all together.

Peaceful resolutions bring peaceful outcomes. Do not rally against. Rally for. Those who oppose have anger in their hearts. Do not be so angry. Anger separates. Anger blocks the power of love. Lovingly embrace your challenges. Lovingly encourage one another.

Forcefully demanding change will bring about more of the same: anger, hatred, desperation. Do not be so angry. Hate fosters fear. Fear triggers war.

Change your world one step at a time, with love as the driving force. Manifest powerful, beautiful outcomes that will bring you peace and harmony.

Be in allowance. Open yourselves up to what is built within you. You have the greatest power to make your world what you wish it to be.

Welcome all possibilities, knowing that whatever is brought before you is brought for you to look at more deeply. Do not be so angry when challenges arise. These are yours to look at. They are presenting themselves to you, as you have brought them to move you into more pleasing directions, to grander opportunities. Learn and improve. This is your innate purpose.

Do not see yourselves as victims in your dysfunctions. You are not such. Victimizing yourselves will keep you where you are, in a place of darkness and non-creativity. This is not who you are. You have free will to move yourselves out of your pains.

Breathe and release this place of judgment. Keep your thoughts light and clear about yourselves and about your world. You are not victims.

Plan your days with love and with the joy of being alive. Live through your soul, for it is calling out to you with every decision that you make. Live your lives with joy in your hearts.

Speak gently. Speak softly. Speak from a loving heart. This will transform you. Kindness will transform the deepest part of you. Assist those who have no love for themselves. Lovingly guide them.

Do your part to help others, for in helping others you are helping yourselves. Be the kindness that you inherently are.

The time is now to realize the importance of raising your vibrations. Participate to activate a higher global frequency. The more of you, the faster, the sooner will you benefit. Your world is affected by your thoughts and your intentions.

The time is now to recognize that you have the power. You are the power that can transform your world.

There is chaos in your world. There is dysfunction. Choose your plan of action wisely.

Send prayers, love, and light to all who are suffering. Send healing to all in crisis. You are all connected. Everything is energy—the greater the vibration, the higher the frequency, the more powerful the impact. Choose to have a positive impact on your world with your thoughts and your intentions.

More and more of your species is awakening to the Divine truth that is within you.

You are experiencing shifts in your consciousness, awakening you to deeper understandings. You are seeing more clearly now. Many of you are using your gifts and abilities in more creative ways to support the ascension of your planet. You are aligning more with your inner soul intelligence, pooling together, finding strength within each other, exercising patience and tolerance for your species, holding more light and spreading it. This is a beautiful reality. We are so very pleased.

Higher frequencies are being poured upon you, assisting your planet in rebalancing itself. Many are experiencing the discomforts that these higher transmissions are creating, as they are adjusting themselves. Do not fear, as this is a process that will bring forth great transformation for all of you. Trust that this is a process—a process of your development.

You will experience discomforts in many ways. There will be feelings and emotions that will arise that will be most difficult. There will be feelings of unresolved painful memories, loss, regret, judgment, extreme sadness, anger, fear ... all what has been buried within you. All of what has been suppressed will present itself. You will be faced with looking at and being with these negative states until you are ready to release them. Trust in this process—this process of your personal evolution and expansion.

Many are feeling much dread and doom, while at the same time experiencing glimpses of bliss and joy. There is inner conflict and competition. Exercise patience and love for yourselves. Allow for all to arise with the knowingness that all shall pass. Do not judge. Be more loving and compassionate as you awaken to the light of who you are. You are shedding the layers upon layers of the old you.

Lovingly embrace this blessing and know that you are guided by a higher intelligence.

Trust that you are on the path of righteousness and self-discovery to assist not only yourselves but your entire world. You are undergoing enormous shifts that will bring forth greater insight and wisdom, which will raise you to new heights and understandings out of your states of depressed anxieties, paving the way to new beginnings for humanity.

Love yourselves. Do not be in judgment. Listen to your body. Give your body what it needs.

Rest when you feel weary. Exert less energy by speaking and doing less. Relax in the peace of nature. Listen to beautiful music. Give yourselves the solitude that you need. Feed your bodies and your minds whatever they are calling out for.

Your body is transforming from the inside out. It needs to rebalance and adjust to the higher frequencies that are offered you. It is vital that you facilitate in this process. Listen to your bodies.

At times, you may believe the imbalance is too great. Trust this is a process. Trust this is energy in motion. Trust this shall pass.

You are guided and supported by a greater power.

Open yourselves up to this truth in order to experience it. Do not close your minds, for then you will block it. Open up to the beauty of who you are and the connectedness to all in existence.

Non-physical beings of higher dimensions are connected to you. We are here to support you. Be in this remembrance and know that you have free will. Ask and only then shall you receive openly and graciously. Be in allowance and embrace the love that you are and the connection that you have to God. You are never alone.

Many will try to assist you by encouraging you to seek professional help, with medications to numb your feelings and emotions. This indeed will not only numb but create even further imbalance. It will block the light of who you are. This will keep you in your dormant states. This is not your answer.

Your answer lies within, with acceptance and allowance of your transformative process to develop. You are evolving and expanding to greater insight and consciousness. Surrender. Be in allowance.

Many will come to you in attempts to shake you out of your depressed state. Embrace it. Love it, for it is the exact opposite.

Your body is allowing for your inner truth to unfold. It is aligning you to the essence of who you truly are, aligning you to your God self. Allow it to unfold naturally.

Be more patient. Be more loving. Be more compassionate with yourselves. This is a beautiful new beginning.

There are many who walk with you, who have been placed on your planet to assist you in your ascension process. They are amongst you. They may be your neighbors, your friends, your co-workers. They are anywhere and everywhere, and they present themselves when they see fit to assist you. Trust that they are amongst you.

You may encounter some by chance, while others may be a constant in your lives. They will lovingly assist you. They are cautious caregivers. They have love in their hearts. They are compassionate souls and have been placed on your planet to assist in your awakening. Their purpose is of a global nature.

Highly empathic ones are here to assist you. They are benevolent souls who carry the wisdom of many lifetimes. They are with you to serve your higher need, to assist in the evolution of your consciousness, to lead the way to higher understandings. Their passion to serve humanity is one to be recognized.

Empaths feel their way through life altering the densities of your planet. They feel your pain. They feel your deeply rooted emotions. They have chosen to absorb and alter these vibrations—to filter, transmute and release them into the light ... into higher frequencies. This is a soul decision.

Be kind to those whom you know. Be kind, for they are enduring much pain and suffering for your species. Love them. Do not be in judgment of their sensitivities.

There are others who walk your planet for shorter periods, lovingly sharing their wisdom, spreading the love that is so much in need. They walk with you. They assist you, and then they move on. These are your Earth angels.

They are sent to you to assist you in seeing the light of who you are. They help you in guiding you to the right places and resources, in accordance with where you are in your development. They encourage you. They support you. Lovingly thank them. They come to you to take you to the next steps in your awakening.

There are many assisting you, planting seeds of higher consciousness within you. Open your hearts and feel this connection, for we are oneness. Feel the Divinity within you.

We have walked on earth, and we understand your pain. We see you. We feel you. We love you and want to help you. We are Divine beings, here to lovingly assist you with the wisdom that is being poured upon you at this time.

We have sent many to assist you. Use what is presented before you. See the opportunity when it comes to you. Look for ways to improve, to heighten your awareness, which will bring you out of your darkness.

We encourage you to open your eyes and see more clearly now. We encourage you to open your hearts and welcome what is being presented to you. We encourage you to live more fully ... to embrace the love that you are ... for you have forgotten.

Come together not only in time of need. Come together as you are one family—the family of God.

Focus on your own development to bring about a global transformation of your planet. Transform yourselves to once again set your lives in proper motion.

Unite in oneness. This is your God-given right. Be in this remembrance when you speak unkindly to others. Be in this remembrance that you are fully creating your new moments, which co-create and co-exist with others. Speak kindly. Be compassionate to one another. Do not be so forthright with that which you speak, for whatever you voice openly cannot be returned.

Be more in this remembrance that you are assisting others in their growth as you are assisting yourselves. Be compassionate with your words, for your words have great power to either enrich or destroy.

Fully understand that it is your responsibility to embrace that which you are and completely and openly extend this beauty to others.

Others are an extension of you. They are no different from you. Love one another. Be kind to one another. Only then can you heal your world. Love is the only way, and it all starts with you. Radiate your light to change your world. This is the only way.

Gentle breeze
Everlasting peace
Birds playfully singing
The song of life

12
Reversing the Dysfunction

Great disturbances are inevitable as you re-align. There will be destruction. Many will perish. Many will falter. Many lives will be taken. Many catastrophes, and much turmoil, anger, frustration, and hatred will be brought up to be cleansed and cleared to make way for the new.

Great shifts will spark and ignite. They will stir what is commonly known. They will transform the fabric of commonality, raising consciousness that has been dormant far too long.

Each day is a new beginning. With each day, begin again. Remember who you are. Keep your focus. Remember that you can change your world by changing yourselves with your attitudes, your beliefs, your words, and your actions, which will change your vibrations. You can change who you are, and who you are in relation to your world. Believe in the power that you are to transform your current situations, to transfer the love that you have to others, to create shifts in your own consciousness.

We love you and lovingly encourage you to begin your own process, which will change everyone and everything around you. The power is within you and the time is now.

Lovingly embrace the power that is within you, for you are the greatest power, for you are a part of God. You have failed to believe this. Believe it, as this is the greatest truth.

When there is no faith, there is no power. Trust in the Divine in you. Trust the essence of who you are to bring realities of beauty, of abundance, of the love that you are, for you are worthy. You are worthy of greatness. You have forgotten. This has become your greatest challenge.

You are limitless beings of light and love. Remember this.

The sky is not the limit. You are beyond this. You are beyond all limitation. Access the truth in you to manifest your greatness to change your world. Cultivate love, for love is All That Is.

Love is the game changer.

The power is within you. Take the time to be with that which you are made of. Take the time to be with the peace within yourselves. Do not be so afraid. Release your fears to the Universe, to Source, to God. Your prayers are heard. Trust and be in allowance for the light in you to ignite and flourish.

We shall repeat the message of truth to you again. This is a book of truths, and the greatest truth is that which you are. You are the essence of love and light. You must be in this remembrance to move forward, to create the greatness that you are. We shall remind you, for you have forgotten.

Save yourselves from the destruction your species has created. Come together. Unite in the oneness of who you are.

Slowly, you will come to this understanding. One at a time, you will join forces with others who have already understood this. There is a vast evolutionary movement that is supporting you. It is expanding the consciousness of humanity, implanting seeds of hope, passion, and ingenuity.

The morality that you have lost will once again be found. All your creations that lack morality will be wiped away, as they will no longer be accepted. More and more of you will implement new ideas that will benefit the collective. All your creations will be out of love, not fear, and will carry the energy of abundance. All will benefit in your new world, not just a few.

It is in your hands to grasp this concept, accept it, and act on it now.

There will be no more suffering, no more pain, nor sorrow. There will be no one left alone, put aside, and forgotten. There will be unity. There will be equality and compassion for all. There will be a universal understanding of who you are and what you can accomplish together. Great shifts will manipulate the energies of your planet and will assist in its healing.

Raise your vibrations to assist in this transformation one step at a time. Take the time to internalize all of what we are putting forth before you. Allow these messages to filter through your beingness and register into your hearts.

Be in this remembrance, for the time is now to facilitate in the process of the evolution of your planet. Fully embrace that which you are. Come together knowing that you are loved.

Set aside your differences. Do not judge one another. Love one another with the differences that you have. Allow each other the space and opportunity for growth. All shall evolve at their own pace when they are ready. You are not responsible for others. You are responsible for yourselves.

Do the best you can to spread the energy of unconditional love. Bless all. Speak less. Listen more. Listen with an open heart. Shine brightly. Be an example for others to follow. Be the light.

Help each other. See past the darkness of your minds. See past the limitations within each other. See each other as the love that you are. This is who you are.

Discover your truth. Look within and reconnect with the Divine in you. Access your power. Embrace the love, kindness, joy, and compassion of that which you are made of. Reconnect.

The time is now.

Mindful awareness is all you need. Be more aware of where you are in your minds. Be more aware to know yourselves.

Create the world you wish to live in. Do not settle for less. Create the abundance you wish to have, for you are deserving of all. Live fearlessly with love in your hearts, and all will come to you. You are vastly supported, each one of you.

Change your minds to change your tomorrows. It is all in your power to do so. The universe is listening. God is listening and working with you.

Use your energy wisely. Focus on all that brings you joy. Rejoice in who you are and who you are becoming, with each day moving closer to the oneness of who you are—moving closer to God. Rejoice, for you are well supported. We are here to encourage you, to show you the way.

Plan and use your logical thinking minds to put your efforts into your most positive uplifting projects. The world is in your hands. Grasp the opportunities that come to you. Do not second guess their authenticity. They are real, and they are yours. The universe is forever giving you these grander opportunities to assist in your advancement.

Follow your passion, and you will not be steered wrongly. Do not allow your pride to stop you from moving forward. You are here for expansion, for growth. You are not meant to remain stagnant.

Fearlessly take risks to bring forth new beginnings. Promote well-being and abundance. Take chances, have faith and trust. Keep moving to create shifts. Move yourselves out of your insecurities, doubts, and fears. Do what pleases you and keep moving forward.

You have incarnated to experience all the joys of life as well as the displeasures. You are here to experience fully moving forward and upward with greater and greater understandings. You are here to evolve. Your future is yours to create.

Take the time to reflect. Choose what you wish for yourselves and your world. You are not separate, as you have continued to believe. Remove what is blocking you. Open your hearts to the oneness of who you are.

Cleanse and clear all obstacles. Remove the stigmas that forbid you and replace them with opportunity and growth, with unity and love. See yourselves as part of a whole, a ball of energy vibrating together. You are creating and co-creating together in the interconnectedness that you are. Remember this, as this is a truth that you must bear.

The vibrational frequency that you emanate affects you all. It affects your moods, your feelings, your emotions, your behaviors, and your physical and emotional wellness.

The time is now to understand this fully, to accept it and to do what you can to make the necessary changes that will bring about more positive outcomes.

Your planet is vibrating at a very low state. As a collective, you are not advancing. You are retracting. More and more are becoming confused, less focused, and more disoriented in the vast chaos of your creations. More and more are feeling the anger, hatred, jealousy, guilt, blame, shame, intolerance, greed, self-righteousness, and divisiveness that your energy is manifesting. More and more are feeling the imbalances of your world.

Know that all is surfacing for you to look at, to process and to evolve from. Embrace it. You are undergoing a process of growth.

The time is now to create a change to help yourselves and your planet. The time is now to raise your vibration, one at a time, and connect with one another in the beauty of who you are. The time is now to foster the glory of who you are, for you are the glory of life. You are the glory of God.

Be in this remembrance and begin now. Do not look back. Look ahead, for only this is real. Create deeply and fully with the passion that comes from deep within you. Be in alignment with your soul. All will fall into place without pain and suffering.

Put aside your doubts and fears. There is no need. Be in allowance and trust. All will fall into place when you have love in your hearts. You will not be steered in a direction that is not pleasing. Your path will be bright with promise, with abundance for all.

Light overpowers darkness. Love and light is your answer.

Exercise more patience. Instant gratification has not served you. All of what is superficial comes all too easily. Your species tends to focus on what brings it momentary pleasures. You bring to you what satisfies your ego selves, not your soul selves.

Realize this for what it is: temporary satisfaction. This is not permanent. This does not bring you the peace that you are longing for. This does not give you the joy of living in your physical states. It is prolonging your suffering.

There is constant comparison and competition amongst you. Your species tends to want things that others have and want these things now. You have no patience. You have no trust. This is pushing you further and further away from the authenticity of who you are. This is pushing you away from God.

Your world is not meant to be used and manipulated. Your species is not meant to have unattainable wants and desires. You are meant to have it all. You have forgotten. We are here to remind you.

The time is now to heal yourselves and your world.

Create the world that you wish to see, where there is no sorrow, no comparison, no competition. Create the world that brings you all that you wish for, all that you desire with justice, equality, compassion, and respect for one another. You are in physicality to create. Do so in loving ways.

Raise your vibrations, to begin your inner transformation, to heal your world.

Promise yourselves. See yourselves as the intuitive intelligence that you are. This is where it all begins. Feel the unconditional, unbinding love you are made of. Live in the truth of who you are to manifest the transformation you wish to see. Bring yourselves back to yourselves. The time is now.

One step at a time, more will unite. There is great hope. Believe this to access it.

Trust that you are where you need to be. Do not look back. Trust that you are in your perfect setting and begin from here. Do not look back in doubt and fear, in loss and disappointment. Start from wherever you are today and move forward by altering your conditioned self with a self-awareness of who you are. Lovingly embrace this beauty. Alter your perception. Your egoic state is not who you are.

You are not your personality. This is a false paradigm. You are not that.

You are not your conditioned self, who has been created over a lifetime of judgment and limitation. You are not that.

You are not your compulsive, negative-thinking minds, which have become that over a lifetime of negative creations.

You are not that which you and others have made yourselves believe. You are much greater.

You are the beauty, the love, and the light of God. You are the essence of All That Is. You are the oneness of God's creations, and you are this connection.

You are not your minds, and you are not your bodies. You are your souls inhabiting your bodies in this lifetime, using them as vehicles from which to experience the creations that you bring forth to your realities, using them to grow and develop from, for your expansion.

You are the soul expression of self. You are the essence that connects you to Divinity.

Your higher self is what is driving you to be better, to be wiser, to have compassion, and to embrace each other, in more loving ways. It is your soul that is encouraging you each second of the day. Stop your busyness long enough to listen and feel with your hearts. Honour yourselves. Feel yourselves into the glory of who you are. You will not be steered wrongly.

Beloved souls in awakening, we promise to deliver all that you need in this time of turbulence. We promise we will never leave you.

Open your hearts to the oneness of who you are. Be in allowance for all of God's love to enter and permeate through your entire beingness, to the core of who you are. Allow Source to enter and take over.

You are not the limitations that you perceive yourselves to be. This is a facade of false beliefs, built like building blocks over a lifetime of pain and suffering. Allow this to pass through you. Allow goodness and love and the light of who you are to enter.

Your creations will glow with Divine intelligence. Your experiences will bring to you all of that which you are yearning. Realize your self-worth. Make this allowance without judgment and uncertainty. Trust in who you are and who you are becoming. Trust that you can heal yourselves and your world with your beliefs, thoughts, and actions. Trust that you are the greatest creators. Transform your world to what you want it to be.

The time is now. Trust in the process.

Do not sit in waiting. Take whatever inspiration comes to you, from wherever it may come, and go wherever it takes you. Follow your inner knowingness of what it is that you may need at this time. You are all at different places in the process of your development. Begin from wherever you need.

Do not follow others and question. You are your own unique self in its perfection. You are not like any other. Trust that you will get closer to the Divinity of who you are, one step at a time. Reconnect with your true nature. Feel your way to the light. You are always guided. Remember and realize the light in you and move forward with faith and with trust.

Do not be afraid that you may not be doing what you should be doing. Do not be so afraid to take the next step. Do not be so confused. Have faith, and you will not be disappointed.

When there is doubt, there is fear. Fear is contraction, not expansion. Move forward fearlessly, and you will be given all that you need to take you to the next steps along your journey.

Proudly announce to yourselves who you are. "I am light. I am love. I am that I am." Repeat this mantra again and again until you believe it, for this is that which you are. Close your eyes and repeat. Do this daily.

Trust in yourselves. You can heal your world. The time is now.

Move forward and never look back. Keep moving forward and upward, keeping your thoughts light, your words soft, and your vision clear. Keep your focus on that which you desire and move forward. Trust the Divine power that you are and watch the magic happen.

Plan your days with the knowingness of who you are. Plan effectively. Bring to you what you are expecting. Remember your truth in its simplicity. Create from this place of wisdom.

The time is now for your species to awaken to your potentiality. You have fallen asleep in the complexities of your creations.

Do not place your focus on that which you do not want. Your species tends to gravitate towards negative discourse. Stop your complaining about what is not working for you. Stop complaining about your life, about others, about events, and about circumstances. Stop all your complaining. This is not serving you. It is keeping you stuck in a place of non-deliverance.

Do not place blame on others. Look within. Start from here. Your lives are in your control. Your world as you see it is in your control. Change your minds and move to a new awareness to create the shifts you are looking for. Try something new. What you as a collective have been doing thus far has not been working.

Bring your planet back to the alignment it needs to function more effectively, to work with you, not against you. Give it the light that it needs to cultivate new beginnings.

Love your life and who you are becoming. Love your species and co-create together the world that you wish to live in, where love is the only vibration. Love will bring you to new heights. Love yourselves and love all around you. Love will bring you what you are seeking.

Bring yourselves together and experience the oneness of who you are—one unified human collective. Create effectively together.

The time is now to stop your complaining and take charge of your lives. You are not alone in this process.

The messages brought forth are simple yet profoundly powerful. They are powerful in their simplicity. We are pleased to deliver them. They are offered you by God.

There is nothing simpler than understanding your true nature and the power that you are. Believe this truth to believe in yourselves. Convince yourselves to move forward. Trust that, with every roadblock, there is a message of hope, of transformation for your higher good.

You will face many obstacles. You will be tested. You will be rocked.

Stay true to your nature. See yourselves as the light. Believe that you are this greatness. Your challenges will remind you of your greatness and stability. As they come, they shall pass. Stay true to the Divine in you. Learn from your experiences and grow through them. You are bringing them to you to do this.

Practice resilience, as does a stream of water to the forces of nature, cleansing and purifying all residue it begets. Practice the peace that you are.

There is no need for conflict. There is no need to prove yourselves right or others wrong. Bless all who come to you with their arguments. Bless them and allow them to be where they are in their own understandings.

See past your egos. Stay true to yourselves. See past the egos of others. This is not who they are. This is fear exemplifying itself fully.

Listen more intently. Breathe more deeply. Respond. Do not react. Remember this, for you will be tested. Allow yourselves growth and expansion.

It is only through your experiences that you may gain greater understandings. Expect miracles, as this is what you are.

There is no mystery. We are providing you with plain and simple truths—truths that you have forgotten. Awaken to endless possibilities. Bring yourselves back to the joy of who you are.

The time is now.

Look around you. See the perfection of life in its creations. See the Divinity in all, for all is of God's creations.

Feel the sadness that permeates your world. Feel the anxiety, the anger, the fear. Feel who you are not. Your species is lost in its pain and suffering. You can change this.

The time is now to awaken to your unlimited potentiality. The time is now to return yourselves to the light in its perfection and lead yourselves into new beginnings, to create the world that you wish to see in its entirety.

Assist in creating the reality that you wish. Create the life that you want. Be the forerunner. Believe in yourselves. Spread the glory of who you are. This is why you came here.

The time has come to awaken.

Release yourselves of your fears, your inhibitions, your limitations. Be fearless. You are limitless. Move forward, fully embracing this truth. Move forward using your minds freely to manifest the world that you wish for ... for it is yours. Transform the false model of who you are not.

You are greatness. You are worthy. You are deserving of all the grace and light of God. Bring back to you that which you truly are.

The time is now.

Do not believe in others to bring about change and opportunity for you. Believe in yourselves.

Do not give yourselves up to others. Your species has allowed itself to be placed in powerless positions. You have allowed yourselves to be fed falsified information. You have allowed yourselves to be stripped of your free will.

You have choice. Believe you are most capable. Believe you are the power. Believe you are the answer. Believe in yourselves.

You have come to your planet in physical form to create, with your free will and choice, which has been lovingly gifted to you by your creator. It is time to reclaim your power, to return to yourselves your free will and create a world that will serve you fully. Take back your power.

Stay strong to the truths that we have brought forth to you.

The time is now to awaken to endless possibilities of who you are in relation to each other and to your world. It is time to pool together and reverse the dysfunction you are living in.

This is not who you are. This is not why you came. You did not come here to be divided. This is not you. This is a false reality—a false version of you. The time is now to return to yourselves your innate power through the loving nature that you are.

You are love. Raise your vibrations to increase awareness that will bring forth unification. Be more conscious to maintain your balance. Be more conscious of what you are transmitting to assist in raising the consciousness of your planet. The time is now.

Focus on what you want for yourselves and for your world. Keep your focus clear, without fear, without doubt, without judgment, without any negativity at all. Trust in what you want. Believe in yourselves that you can attain it. Keep your focus clear, your thoughts light, and your words compassionate.

Find ways to help yourselves and encourage others to do the same. Help one another with love in your hearts.

Your world is under transformation. Assist your home in this process.

Shift the energy of your planet to new heights, to new awareness, insight, and knowledge, to new beginnings. Assist in creating a lighter model of life on your planet. The time is now.

You have been in waiting far too long. Grasp what is yours and change your world to be the best it can be. Proudly proclaim your right to readjust and realign the old model, which has not been effectively working for you for millennia.

You are one with God. Unite in this oneness. Stand strong in unison. More and more will follow. Have no doubt. You are fully supported by Source.

Rocky Road
Confusion, Separation
Isolation

Hatred, Anger, Fear
Darkness

Who am I?

Awakening Truth
Clarity, Unity
Resolution

Love, Peace, Harmony
Light

13
The Shift Is Happening

The time has come to rise together and take a stand for justice and equity for all. The time has come to take part in this great movement towards unification.

The awakening process is happening, and it is happening for all of you. Believe this, as this is the truth. Choose to willingly participate. Do not resist. Know in your hearts that you are being guided for transcendence.

Your beliefs have not served you. They have created divisions amongst you. They have contributed to the heart-breaking condition of your planet. They have altered your natural state. They have compromised the fabric of your existence.

It is time to step out of this disharmony and step into deeper understandings that will bring forth grandeur opportunities and realities. It is time to join with those who have the same vision—the vision of a world that will support you all. It is time to unite in oneness and do your part.

Put aside your differences. Put aside your hurts and your pain. Create a world that is free from heartache and sorrow. Fully embrace and rejoice in the gifts, talents, and abilities that have been offered you and use them in ways that will benefit all. Raise the vibration of your planet.

Realize your greatness and stand strong in unison, peacefully forging forward and upward with love as your driving force. Live your lives in the present moment connected to your hearts.

You are not alone on this journey. Follow God. You have not been forgotten.

Rejoice in this understanding and proclaim to experience life through your soul self. Align yourselves with your true selves to experience the highest model of yourselves. This will change your world.

We encourage you to open to new possibilities and opportunities. We encourage you to let go of all that you are carrying, all that is weighing heavily upon you—all that is suppressing your freedom. Put aside your differences. Put aside your ego selves. Believe in the unity of who you are, not in the separation. You are not separate beings.

Create a world free from the suffering states that you have placed on yourselves. Begin from wherever it is that you are with the understanding it is your responsibility to begin your own process of transformation.

Rejoice in who you are and who you are becoming. Rejoice that you are supreme beings. Honor the Godly nature in you. Harness your intuitive intelligence that is awaiting you.

Create the world you wish to live in with purity, innocence, and love for one another—for all. Create your new world now.

Understand you have been fed mistruths about who you are as attempts in keeping you stuck and immobile, and paralyzed in fear. You have been locked in a suppressed state and been given glimpses of growth to keep you hopeful for more.

Living in this powerless state, hoping and trusting others to do the work for you ... others to keep order for you, others to make you well again, others to bring you peace again, others to fix things for you, is not who you are.

There is no need to hand over your power to others. There is no need to look elsewhere. You are the greatest power of all, for you are Divinity in its creation. Believe this to actualize it.

Stay true. Stay focused on that which you are wanting. Trust and believe you are fully supported by the universe. Ask with an open and loving heart and you shall receive.

Do not doubt, for doubt is the energy of fear. Release this, as this is blocking your growth, progression, and expansion. Release all forms of fear. You have nothing to fear. Release that which is forbidding your expansion, contracting your intuitive flow.

Fear is what is blocking you. Doubt is what is blocking you. Do not set limitations before you.

Stand strong and be fearless to create what you really want ... openly, humbly accepting the beauty of the Divine in you. You are fearless in nature. Remember this to bring this back to yourselves, for this is what you are. Fearlessly create new beginnings.

You are infinite beings of light. Remember this truth, for this is your truth.

Your world as you know it is in dysfunction with your belief in separation and your mindless creations. Your world is crumbling before you. Awaken to this reality. Awaken to the truth before you. Understand that you have contributed to this madness. Understand you can change this.

Look around you. Notice the injustice in your world. Really take notice. This is what is real right now.

Your world is suffering. You are all suffering, and you are suffering from what you are doing and what you have been doing to each other and to your home.

Your species has lost the kindness and compassion that you are made of. You have lost yourselves in your dysfunction, in your competitiveness and self-righteousness. This is not who you are. It is time to start thinking for yourselves. It is time to start following your hearts.

Join forces with those who are on a more elevated path, one which does not exclude but includes all. Unite as one and move forward. Take a stand, firmly supporting all who have love in their hearts, all who emanate purity and light, all who speak of love as the energy that will bring you together.

Love is the answer.

Your system of divisiveness is gouging the deepest hole amongst you. It is creating much unnecessary pain and suffering.

The time has come to restructure your world. You have the power to create a new, lighter world, one that is more to your liking. You have the power to create a new world of peaceful existence, whereby all are treated equally, all are respected, and all are cared for.

This is your vision, and this is where you are heading. Trust in yourselves in the greatness that you are. You are on a journey towards higher understandings. New beginnings will foster new growth.

Begin your process of recreating your world. The time is now.

Demonstrate what it is that you wish for. Demonstrate together. Pool together and demonstrate. Take action. Empower yourselves and move forward. Few are ruling you. You are many. You are the collective.

Demonstrate what you wish for peacefully. Demonstrate for, rather than against. Anger will bring more of the same. It will foster hatred, that which you are not. Demonstrate with love and compassion, and who you are will surface, glow, and flow. You are well supported.

There is no better time than now. This is your time.

Help each other. Find your power by empowering others. Align yourselves with your authentic power and support those who have fallen asleep. One at a time, do your part in raising the vibration of your planet. Support your nations that feel they have been forgotten. Unite and assist in transforming the energy that is holding them hostage. Show them the way, for there is another way. Help each other out of your misery.

You are one family living together in one home, that which you call Earth. See yourselves as the family that you are and begin from here.

Move forward accepting the challenge that has been brought forth to you. Take responsibility and trust that you will be rewarded. The universe responds in most expansive ways to whatever you are transmitting.

Do not hesitate. Do not forget. Join in the planetary shift that is happening now. Transmute the energy of your planet. Assist in raising global awareness. Assist in bringing the light that you are back to yourselves, for you are the light, the light of God. Resist no further.

Accept the challenge and re-awaken your planet. The time is now.

Love who you are and who you are becoming. Love that you are a part of this movement. Allow yourselves to be that and love who you are.

Encourage one another, as there is hope.

Shine your light to influence others. Shine brightly. Assist in the transformation that your planet needs. Your species needs assistance. Be of that. Help each other. Care for others as you care for yourselves. You are one in the same.

Save yourselves to save your world.

Spread the word of Divine wisdom of hope and love that will transform you. Spread the knowledge that you have. Keep your focus and direct your intention on what matters most. Live in the truth of who you really are, and you will greatly be rewarded.

Forgive all who have wronged you. Forgiveness will elevate your consciousness. Forgive yourselves and forgive others. Allow the energy of love to flow through you and out to each one of you. Release the fear and doubt and be comforted in knowing that for-giveness will transform you. Release the burden of hostility that plagues you. Release the anger, the guilt, and the blame. Forgive all, and you will greatly be rewarded.

The time is now to fully accept the transformation of your planet, allow the shift to flow with ease, and accelerate its speed with your willingness and intention.

The time is now to take charge of your lives and where it is heading. Take charge. You are in control. The power is within you to make your lives what you want them to be. You are in total control. Have this awareness to step forward into your next chapter—your most rewarding one. Begin now.

There is a new generation of healers and light workers who are working with you. You have great support systems in place for you. Many will come to you to assist you when you are ready.

Open to the truth of the greatness that you are. Reclaim your power.

Raise the vibration of your planet. Let go of the density you are carrying. Raise yourselves.

Remember who you are. Heal your world.

You are the essence of light and love. Remember this truth as the greatest truth of all.

We love you, and we leave you with this.

Epilogue

Channeled Message from Ascended Masters:

We are pleased you have taken the time to read this material. We are grateful in offering you our guidance and hopeful you have absorbed what it is in need at this time.

We wish for you to recognize you all have Divinity within you. You are all supported by spirit. It is for you to recognize this and work within it if you so choose.

One step at a time, one moment at a time, you will notice changes within you that will impact on decisions you make in your lives and influence you greatly. We commend you for your courage in making these changes, in altering your belief systems, one at a time. We commend you in wanting to help yourselves to be the best version of yourselves, and to ultimately help each other and your planet.

We encourage you to keep this read close to you and re-read it as often as you need, as a reminder of who you are, and with each time, gain a new perspective as you continue on your evolutionary process.

Thank you dear ones. We love you.

In Closing

Thank you for being a part of my journey, for taking the time to read what has inspired me and impacted my life greatly.

If this read has stirred you in some way, it has brought you closer to opening the doors of opportunity which lie ahead. We all want the same. We all want to live our lives without stress and struggle. We all want peace. There is a commonality amongst us that binds us. My hope is for you to choose to remember this and hold the intention of healing our world.

God bless you in finding your truth and awakening to the light of who you are, the love that will change our world and bring us all together.

For information about special discounts on bulk purchases to your company, for educational purpose, reselling, book clubs, fundraiser campaigns or gifts, or information about booking speaking engagements, please contact me at 1-416-473-4325 or jalexopoulos1955@gmail.com

You may also follow me at Facebook.com/Awakentoyourtruth111 and Instagram @joannaalexopoulos.

But please don't follow me on Twitter. I'm embarrassed to admit I'm not the best at tweeting. My kids will attest to that.

My website is www.awaken-to-your-truth.com

Acknowledgements

I would like to thank God for the on-going support offered ever so lovingly by His Divine family of spirit guides, angels and archangels whom I call upon daily, who guide, support, and encourage me to be the best I can be. They have shown me the greatness of who we are and the connection that we all have to the Divine in us.

I would like to thank the benevolent entities of Abadania, Brazil who created a great shift in me, who lifted the veil of darkness and shed light on the truth of who I really am, who took me through to the next steps one at a time, regaining the trust that I had lost, the trust in myself as a healer, a child of God.

A special thank you to the ascended masters, who have spoken through me in writing this book, humbly offering their loving wisdom, to assist in the awakening process of humanity. Words cannot express the gratitude I feel for being of such service to God.

I would like to thank my dear husband who has supported me throughout the trials and tribulations of my evolutionary journey. George has been a constant in my life and has shown me the way, leading by example, reminding me of the beauty of life—of the love that exceeds all. His laughter and gentle, loving, compassionate heart provide me with comfort. He is my soul mate, my best friend.

Thank you to my children, Dimitri and Chris. I thank them for their support in challenging times, for the unconditional love that they have always shown me, and for the life lessons that I have learned through them in parenthood.

I would like to express gratitude to all who have come into my life, both from childhood and adulthood, for short periods and longer. Thank you for bringing what I needed to see to the light. Thank you for showing me what I needed to learn. Thank you for bringing me what I needed when I needed it, all assisting in my growth, all helping me to release what I needed, helping me to put aside my ego, to forgive myself and others, and to get out of my way and let God lead me. I am continuing to learn from my relationships and I am eternally grateful for all that has presented itself through these.

Thank you to all the inspiring teachers who have shown me the way, who have taught me about life and beyond—about energy, vibration and frequency. Thank you to Eckhart Tolle, Louise Hay, Maryann Williamson, Neale Donald Walsch, Matt Kahn, James Van Praagh, Judith Orloff, Deepak Chopra, Doreen Virtue, Esther and Jerry Hicks and Caroline Myss. Thank you also to Bruce Lipton who is working tirelessly bridging the gap between science and spirituality for those of us who still question.

And finally, a special thank you to Oprah Winfrey, who has opened gateways of communication, connecting these teachers to humanity, spreading the joy of life, and the word of God.

Printed in Canada